Indiana ISTEP+ Reading Coach, Grade 3

by
Stuart Margulies, Ph.D.,
Maria Goudiss,
& Judith Lechner

Educational Design

EDI 520

ACKNOWLEDGMENTS

Aesop, "The Crow and the Pitcher," "The Wolf and the Sheep."

Avena, Theresa, "Life in the New World." Printed by permission of the author.

Dean, Pamela, "Out the Window." Printed by permission of the author.

Flame, Heather, "Two Boys." Printed by permission of the author.

Miranda, Eddie, "Life in Indiana." Printed by permission of the author.

For information about permission, write to:
Educational Design, 345 Hudson Street, New York, NY 10014-4502

ISBN# 0-87694-967-7   EDI 520

10 9 8 7 6 5 4 3 2

TABLE OF CONTENTS

TO THE TEACHER

This book is primarily aimed at the development of higher-order reading competencies for beginning third-grade students. It is aligned with Indiana Academic Standards. *The Indiana Reading and Language Arts Coach Grade 3* is intended to provide the teacher with the necessary supporting material to help teach the reading and language arts academic standards. *The Coach* also helps prepare the student for the Indiana Reading Tests, including the **ISTEP+**. It focuses on comprehension strategies, usage competencies, and the skills required to synthesize information from a variety of sources.

A detailed listing of the Indiana Academic Standards for English/Language Arts is found in the Teacher's Guide.

Students must read and analyze a wide range of genres and must demonstrate proficiency in reading comprehension, as well as prepare written answers to writing prompts. The four Review sections employ answer modes similar to those found on the Indiana Reading Tests. Sometimes students are given three choices and sometimes four, just like on the tests.

Selections on the Indiana Reading Tests range from simple to difficult. Some questions assess the literal or recall level of reading performance, but most questions require higher order reading skills, in accord with the Indiana Academic Standards. *The Coach* develops the full spectrum of reading levels, but most attention is directed to higher-level skills.

Selections included in this book match Indiana Reading Tests item profiles. They have been chosen for their high interest level. Students benefit most when they can read the stories at a relaxed pace and have plenty of time for classroom discussion.

We hope and expect not only that students will enhance their reading competencies, but that they will also enjoy the reading selections.

TO THE STUDENT

This book will help you to become a better reader and writer. It will also help you do well on the Indiana Reading Tests. *The Coach* gives you practice and hints that will help you answer many different kinds of questions. Sometimes you will have to choose from three possible answers and sometimes from four, just like on the tests.

We hope you like the stories.

PART 1: WORD RECOGNITION AND RESEARCH STRATEGIES

In this part of **The Indiana Reading Coach**, you will learn how to recognize, understand, and pronounce words.

You will use:

- phonics,

- knowledge of word parts, and

- knowledge of the meaning of other words.

With these tools, you can work out how words sound and what they mean.

Third graders read many different kinds of books. *The Coach* will give you many tips on how to read books better.

Lastly, you will learn some study skills and how to find information you need.

1 WORDS THAT SOUND THE SAME

VOWELS

You know already how most **vowels** sound. You know how to pronounce:

> the *a* in *bat*
>
> the *e* in *met*
>
> the *i* in *tip*
>
> the *o* in *crops*
>
> the *u* in *nut*

You may be asked about some other common vowel sounds. Here are some of them:

> The sound of *a* in *male*
> The sound of *ai* in *fail*
>
> The sound of *ee* in *feel*
> The sound of *ie* in *piece*
> The sound of *ea* in *leaf*
>
> The sound of *oo* in *boot*
>
> The sound of *oo* in *foot*
>
> The sound of *oi* in *coil*
> The sound of *oy* in *joy*

The sound of <u>ou</u> in <u>loud</u>

The sound of <u>ow</u> in <u>howl</u>

The sound of <u>au</u> in <u>haul</u>

The sound of <u>aw</u> in <u>crawl</u>

The sound of <u>al</u> in <u>call</u>

Notice that some of the phrases above are printed close together. This means that the underlined vowels sound the same, even though they are spelled differently. *Coil* and *joy* have the same vowel sounds, even though one sound is spelled *oi* and one is spelled *oy*.

Notice that the words *boot* and *foot* look very much alike, but their vowels sound different.

Read the sentence in Example 1. Then decide which word has the same vowel sound as the word in the sentence.

Example 1

Please don't be *late*.

1   **Which word has the same vowel sound as *late*?**

   A   latch

   B   march

   C   rail

The correct answer is C. Notice that the vowel in *rail* is spelled *ai*, but it sounds the same as the vowel in *late*.

Example 2

My *foot* hurts.

2 Which word has the same vowel sound as *foot*?

  A food

  B shoot

  C wood

The correct answer is C. The vowel sound in *wood* is the same as the vowel sound in *foot*.

Example 3

He says that it's not his *fault*.

3 Which word does NOT have the same vowel sound as *fault*?

  A haul

  B howl

  C shawl

The correct answer is B. The vowels in the other two words sound the same as the vowel in *fault*. But the vowel in *howl* sounds different.

WORDS

There are many words that sound exactly the same but have different meanings. (These words are called **homophones**.) Here are some of them:

Brake	Break	
Fare	Fair	
Hear	Here	
Led	Lead (the metal)	
Peace	Piece	
Their	There	
To	Too	Two
Weak	Week	

If you hear your teacher use one of these words, you may not be sure which word is being used. But there's a way to solve this problem. If you listen to the rest of the sentence, you can usually work out what it means.

If a friend says:

Would you like a *piece* of this pie?

You could tell that *piece* means "a part." You wouldn't think it means "quiet" (*peace* and quiet)!

When you guess which word is being used from the rest of the sentence, we call it **using context clues**.

Use context clues to work out the meaning of the word *fare* in the next example.

Example 4

4 **In which sentence can the blank be replaced by the word *fare* (NOT the word *fair*)?**

A The _____ is coming to town tonight.

B Here is some money to pay your _____.

C It's not _____ to me if I only get half.

 Your teacher will discuss your answer.

HELPFUL HINTS FOR WORDS THAT SOUND THE SAME

1. Listen carefully to the sound that vowels make.

2. Some words have the same vowel sound even though they are spelled differently.

3. Use context clues to figure out the meaning of words that sound the same but mean different things (homophones).

SELECTIONS FOR PRACTICE

Read each selection and answer the question or questions. Each answer choice has a bubble in front. Fill in the bubble next to the best choice.

Selection 1

Each disk costs $15.

1 **Which word has the same vowel sound as *each*?**

- O fetch
- O peel
- O search

Selection 2

My mother is very *proud* that I passed the test.

2 **Which word has the same vowel sound as *proud*?**

- O book
- O down
- O four

Selection 3

You can stop a door from squeaking if you *oil* its hinges.

3 **Which word has the same vowel sound as *oil*?**

- O boy
- O crow
- O more

Selection 4

Help yourselves to ice cream. Then we can play *ball*.

4   **Which word has the same vowel sound as *ball*?**

- O   barn
- O   fall
- O   male

Selection 5

5   **In which sentence can the blank be replaced by the word *week* (NOT the word *weak*)?**

week = seven days
weak = not strong

- O   He's a _____ leader; he can't make decisions.
- O   She has a _____ ankle.
- O   We spent a _____ at the beach.

Selection 6

6   **In which sentence can the blank be replaced by the word *blew* (NOT the word *blue*)?**

- O   Color the sea in the picture _____ .
- O   The wind _____ the newspaper away.
- O   The _____ jay is a very common bird.

2 UNDERSTANDING THE MEANING OF WORDS

GUESSING THE MEANING OF A WORD FROM THE WORDS AROUND IT

As you read, you may come across a word you don't know. You may be able to figure out what the word means by seeing how it is used.

For example:

> That is *artificial* ice cream.

Do you know what *artificial* means? You can't figure it out from this sentence. But you can figure out what it means if you read the whole paragraph.

> That is *artificial* ice cream. It doesn't have any real cream in it. It is made from fish and plants. It doesn't taste nearly as good as real ice cream.

Have you figured out what *artificial* means? *Artificial* means "fake" or "not natural." The second sentence gave a good clue. "It doesn't have any real cream in it." *Real* is the opposite of *artificial*.

Whenever you see a new word, look at how it is used. Look at the other words in the sentence. Look at the sentences before and after the new word. As you learned in the previous chapter, this is called using context clues.

Read the next example and figure out the meaning of the word *savage* from the context.

Example 1

Frank acts like a *savage* in the lunchroom. He grabs food. He eats with his hands. He won't use a knife and fork. And he pushes people so he can get to the front of the line.

1   **A *savage* is**

   A   a wild person

   B   an honest person

   C   a shy person

The correct choice is A, *a wild person*. You read how Frank acted. He doesn't act like a friend. He doesn't act like a shy person or an honest person. He is a wild person. You figured out what *savage* means from the context.

Try the next example.

Example 2

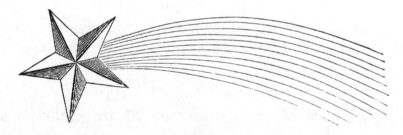

Rashan thinks the stars are beautiful. He can *gaze* at them for hours. He likes to visit his uncle in the country. At night the sky there is black, so he can really see the stars well.

2 **A person who *gazes* at the stars**

    A dislikes them

    B draws them

    C looks at them

 Your teacher will discuss your answer.

PREFIXES AND SUFFIXES

Look at these words.

    Unknown   Uncertain   Impolite   Impossible

Two of these words begin with **un**. The two other words begin with **im**. **Un** and **im** are **prefixes**.

When either **un** or **im** is put before a word, it means the opposite of the word, or "not."

    Unknown means "not known."

    Uncertain means "not certain."

    Impolite means "not polite."

    Impossible means "not possible."

Prefixes are put in front of words to change the meaning of the words.

Read the next story and decide on the meaning of the underlined word.

Example 3

Gina was always alone. She didn't like to talk to anyone. Sometimes she would frown when people asked her to play. She was very <u>unfriendly</u>.

3 **Someone who is *unfriendly* doesn't like**

A bicycles

B people

C vacations

B is the correct choice. Someone who is unfriendly doesn't like to be around people.

Prefixes go in front of words, but **suffixes** are put at the end of words. Suffixes often take words that mean an activity like "dance" or "run," and turn them into words that mean a person who does that activity, like "dancer" or "runner."

So **er** is often used to do this. So is **ist**, in words like *typist*, which means "someone who types."

When you see a word ending in **er** or **ist**, the selection is talking about a person who does something. If you read the word without the **er** or **ist** ending, you can tell what the person does.

Example 4

Sally couldn't play the piano or guitar. She was only good at the trumpet and the saxophone. But she was the best flutist I've ever heard.

4   **Sally was good at playing the**

   A   piano

   B   flute

   C   trumpet

   Your teacher will discuss your answer.

PHRASES

Sometimes you must figure out what a **phrase** of two or more words means.

Read Example 5 and figure out the meaning of *accurate shooter*.

Example 5

Most basketball players are tall. Bunny Levitt was very short. But Bunny was a good shot. He almost never missed. He could throw a ball into the basket almost every time.

In 1935, there was a contest. Bunny threw the ball into the basket 499 times. He didn't miss once. He was the most *accurate shooter* who ever lived. No one is as good a shooter as Bunny.

5   **An *accurate shooter***

   A   likes to play basketball

   B   almost never misses when he shoots the ball

   C   must be tall

   Your teacher will discuss your answer.

21

CHOOSING THE WORD THAT MAKES SENSE

Some stories have missing words. You have to fill in the blank with the word that makes the most sense.

Example 6

Fred is eating bread and _____.

6   **Pick the word that makes the most sense.**

A   rocks

B   butter

C   pants

The correct choice is B. That makes sense. Fred wouldn't eat rocks or pants.

HELPFUL HINTS FOR UNDERSTANDING THE MEANING OF A NEW WORD OR PHRASE

1. Read the sentence with the new word or phrase.

2. Read the sentences before and after the word or phrase.

3. Guess what the word means from the context.

4. Look at the answers. Pick the choice closest to what you guessed.

5. Look at the beginning or end of the underlined word. See if it has a prefix or suffix. If the word has a prefix with *un* or *im*, you know this means the opposite. If the word has a suffix with *er* or *ist*, you know it refers to a person who does something.

6. When you have to fill in a blank, pick the word that makes the most sense.

SELECTIONS FOR PRACTICE

Read each selection and answer the question or questions. Each answer choice has a bubble in front. Fill in the bubble next to the best choice.

Selection 1

Mrs. Lopez watched her dog run into the street. A truck came racing toward her pet. Mrs. Lopez was *terrified*. The truck missed her dog at the last second. Mrs. Lopez felt sick all day. It had been very close.

1   *Terrified* **means**

- O   happy
- O   lonely
- O   scared

Selection 2

The diamond was very large. But it wasn't worth a lot. It didn't shine the way it should. It was imperfect.

2   **When something is *imperfect*, it**

- O   has something wrong with it
- O   is very valuable
- O   isn't large enough

Selection 3

Ramon has a new job. He works very hard. He lifts heavy boxes all day. At the end of the day, he is *exhausted*. He has to have a nap before dinner.

3 **You have read that Ramon was *exhausted* from doing hard work. Who else would probably be *exhausted*?**

- a boy who eats an apple
- a person who reads a newspaper
- a woman who runs 30 miles

Selection 4

Mr. and Mrs. Patel always *obey the law*. They always stop at red lights. They always wear seat belts when they are in the car. They try to do what the laws say they should do.

4 **A person who *obeys the law***

- doesn't understand the law
- often breaks the law
- follows the law

Selection 5

My cousin ran 20 miles today. Afterward he was very ____. He slept for ten hours that night.

- tired
- clean
- angry

3 | READING A VARIETY OF MATERIALS

THE PURPOSE OF A BOOK AND INTENDED AUDIENCE

Information can be found in many different places. The books you use in your classroom teach you a lot about reading, math, and social studies. The instructions that come with toys and computers tell you how to make them work.

There are all kinds of reasons why we read. Authors have all kinds of purposes for writing books. Here are some of them:

- Non-fiction passages and newspapers tell us facts.

- Instructions tell us how to do something.

- Stories and poetry can be fun to read. We enjoy meeting the characters, sharing their adventures, and being happy or sad with them.

- Some newspaper and magazine articles may try to get us to think a certain way or do something differently.

When you read a passage, you can usually work out what its purpose is. Read the passage in Example 1. Then decide what it is trying to do.

Example 1

Cut a banana in half. Put three scoops of ice cream on the banana. Put chocolate sauce on top of the ice cream. Add whipped cream. Add nuts and three cherries.

1A   **What is the purpose of these sentences?**

A   to make you laugh

B   to make you agree with the author

C   to tell you how to do something

The correct answer is C, *to tell you how to do something*. These are instructions for how to make an ice cream sundae.

Now think about where you might find these instructions on making a dessert.

1B   **Where might you find these sentences?**

A   in a cookbook

B   in a sports magazine

C   in a book about zoo animals

 Your teacher will discuss your answer.

COMPARE AND CONTRAST STORIES OR BOOKS WITH SIMILAR TOPICS

Sometimes we compare different kinds of stories or books with similar topics.

Read the next two passages and answer the question.

Example 2

LIFE IN INDIANA

by Eddie Miranda

My family and I came to Gary, Indiana from Puerto Rico. Here it is more exciting. You can meet more people. There are more places to go. There are many different things to do. That makes life more interesting and exciting. You can have a better life here. But I don't know if we'll stay.

Life here is different. The climate of Puerto Rico is better. It is much warmer there. You can spend more time outside and the winter wasn't so bad.

> *climate = type of weather*

School is very hard. The language is different, the teachers are rushed, and the whole approach is different. Because school is so hard, we have many problems.

In spite of everything, we still like it here. My father has a good job. My mother works, too. We have many things we never had before, like a TV and many clothes. I am happy to be in the United States of America.

FINDING A LIFE IN THE NEW WORLD

By Theresa Avena

I was nine when I came to America. My father wanted to leave Italy. We had very little food. My father knew that he could find work in the United States. He wanted to be able to live well. He wanted to save money and buy a house.

My first day at school wasn't much fun. The kids all stared at me. I couldn't speak any English, and no one spoke Italian. I didn't know how to tell the teacher I needed to use the bathroom. It was horrible.

I couldn't eat the food. There was nothing I liked and I didn't like how it smelled. I wanted to go home very badly.

Slowly my English got better. I made some friends. They made school fun.

I studied very hard. I got very good grades. I went to college. Now I'm a teacher and I try to help new students. Being a teacher is wonderful. My family is proud of me. America has been good to me.

2 **How do these passages compare?**

A They are both about people who were new to this country.

B They are both about life in Puerto Rico.

C They are both about going to college.

 Your teacher will discuss your answer.

LOOKING AT PICTURES

Pictures often tell you about the story.

Look at the next picture. See if you can guess what the story is about.

Example 3

3 **What do you think this story is mostly about?**

A a woman who won a race

B men and women who are very strong

C the fastest horse in the world

The correct choice is A. The picture shows three women running a race. None of the other choices is correct. If the story were about horses, a different picture would have been used.

Read the next passage. Then pick the picture that goes best with the story.

Example 4

Arthur and his cousin Barry are very different. Barry likes to play the guitar. But Arthur likes almost any sport. He plays baseball, basketball, and soccer.

4   **Pick the picture that goes with the story.**

A   Picture 1

B   Picture 2

C   Picture 3

D   Picture 4

    Your teacher will discuss your answer.

READING THE INTRODUCTION TO A STORY

Many stories begin with an **introduction**. The introduction tells you what the story is about.

Look at the picture. Then read the introduction.

See if you can decide what the selection will be about.

Example 5

Roses

INTRODUCTION

Roses are beautiful flowers. Some roses grow wild. Others need a lot of care. Some roses are bright red. Others are yellow. There is even a black rose.

5 **What do you think this selection will be about?**

A the many different kinds of roses

B flowers that grow inside houses

C different kinds of soils

D how to raise butterflies

The best answer is A. The introduction and the picture tell us that the story will be about the many different kinds of roses.

USING YOUR OWN KNOWLEDGE

Another way to understand what you read is to use what you know.

For example, you have seen how people act when they get lost. You have seen how people act when they get a nice birthday gift. What you know about people may help you understand why people in stories act the way they do.

Read Example 6. Decide what was wrong with Fred in this story.

Example 6

> Fred coughed. Then he sneezed. His head hurt. His mother said he had a fever. She told him to go to bed. Then she gave him some juice to drink. Fred stayed home and slept. He felt terrible.

6   **What do you think was wrong with Fred?**

    A   He was feeling nervous.

    B   He had a bad cold.

    C   He was tired from playing too much.

    D   He ate too much.

 Your teacher will discuss your answer.

UNDERSTANDING SIGNS

Every day you see **signs** all around you. When you ride in a car or bus, you see signs that look like this:

When you see this sign, you know the car or bus will stop.

You see other signs like these:

Look at these signs. Figure out what each one means. Then answer the question.

Example 7

7 There is a hole in the road. Which of these signs would tell the driver to be very careful?

A Sign 1

B Sign 2

C Sign 3

D Sign 4

If you chose B, you are correct. A DANGER sign warns of road problems.

IDENTIFYING NEEDED INFORMATION FROM CHARTS AND SCHEDULES

Sometimes information is put into **chart** form. A chart has at least two columns. Each column has a heading. The heading tells you what the information in the column is about.

You will find charts in your textbooks. You can make charts to compare things.

Look at this chart comparing frogs and fish.

FROGS	FISH
live on land and in water	live in water only
swim in water; hop on land	swim in water
breathe with lungs	breathe with gills
have legs	have fins

Now answer the question based on what you read on the chart.

Example 8

8   **Which of these sentences is true?**

    A   Frogs live only in the water.

    B   Fish breathe with gills.

    C   Frogs can't hop.

    D   Frogs have fins.

Only Choice B is true. Look under the heading *Fish* to see how they breathe.

Schedules are a kind of chart. Schedules tell you what to do at what time. They also tell you when a bus or train is coming.

Read this schedule. Then answer the question.

Example 9

SCHOOL BUS LEAVES FOREST ROAD	SCHOOL BUS RETURNS TO FOREST ROAD
7:00 A.M.—High School	2:05 P.M.— High School
7:35 A.M.—Middle School	2:45 P.M.— Middle School
8:10 A.M.—Grades 2 to 4	3:35 P.M.— Grades 2 to 4

9   **If you are in Grade 3 and live near Forest Road, when do you get the bus to school in the morning?**

    A   at 7:00 A.M.

    B   at 7:35 A.M.

    C   at 8:10 A.M.

    D   at 3:35 P.M.

 Your teacher will discuss your answer.

HELPFUL HINTS FOR READING AND UNDERSTANDING A VARIETY OF MATERIALS

1. Read the selection and decide what its purpose is. Does it give facts or tell you how to do something? Is it meant for fun and enjoyment? Is the purpose to get you to think a certain way or do something?

2. A selection often has clues that help you understand it.
   - Stories may have helpful **introductions**.
   - Stories and articles may have pictures that tell you more about what is happening in the text.

3. What you know about people can help you understand why people in stories act the way they do.

4. When you compare passages, ask yourself how they are alike and how they are different.

5. **Signs** use words and pictures to send a message. Learn what everyday signs mean.

6. **Charts** and **schedules** contain important information. Both have columns. Each column has a heading that shows its topic. Use the headings to find the information you want.

SELECTIONS FOR PRACTICE

Read each selection and answer the question or questions. Each answer choice has a bubble in front. Fill in the bubble next to the best choice.

Selection 1

Public School 68's Drama Club invites you to a show this Wednesday at 7:00 P.M. The show is Mary Poppins. Tickets are $3. Free cookies during the break. Everyone is welcome.

1   **Where would you probably read these sentences?**

- O   in a school social studies book
- O   in the telephone book
- O   on a school bulletin board

Selection 2

HOW TO USE THE COPY MACHINE

PRESS THE LARGE **ON** BUTTON.

PRESS **REGULAR** PAPER OR **LONG** PAPER.

SET THE NUMBER OF COPIES YOU WANT.

PRESS THE GREEN **START** BUTTON.

2   **Why did the author write these lines?**

- O   to tell who invented the copy machine
- O   to explain how to do something
- O   to help people enjoy what they're reading

Selection 3

The next time you put a battery in a toy, be careful. Look inside the place that holds the battery. You'll see a + sign at one end and a - sign at the other end. The battery also has a + sign at one end and a - sign at the other. Put the battery in so that its + end is at the + end of the place that holds it. The toy may not work if you don't do this.

3 **What did the author want readers to know?**

O   how to put a battery in a toy

O   why some toys are dangerous

O   why some toys need batteries

Selection 4

INTRODUCTION

Gold miners searched for gold pieces in streams. They used special tools to find the gold. If they found gold, they were always very happy. They would become rich.

4 **What do you think this selection will be about?**

O   camping

O   looking for gold

O   fishing in streams

Selection 5

Many people think Satchel Paige was the best pitcher in baseball history. Because he was black, he was not allowed to play in the Major Leagues for many years. He was middle aged when he finally got to play in the Majors.

Leroy Paige, or "Satchel" Paige, as he was called, grew up at a time when black players were not let in the Major Leagues. Most of his career was spent pitching for black baseball teams, where he was a great star.

Late in his career, the Major Leagues finally began to have black players on their teams. Satchel Paige was one of the first black pitchers to be signed. He entered the Majors at an age when most players have already retired. He pitched in the Majors for many years.

He was still good enough to be brought back to pitch when he reached the age of 59. This made him the oldest pitcher in baseball history. If he'd joined the Major Leagues at the usual age of 19 or 20, he might have broken all the records in Major League pitching history.

5A The introduction tells you that

- ○ Satchel Paige's real name was Leroy
- ○ Satchel Paige broke many Major League records
- ○ Satchel Paige was one of the greatest pitchers of all time
- ○ Satchel Paige started playing baseball when he was very young

5B What do you learn about Satchel Paige from the picture?

- ○ He wore a beard.
- ○ He liked to joke around.
- ○ He always touched the ground before he pitched a ball.
- ○ He played for New York.

Selection 6

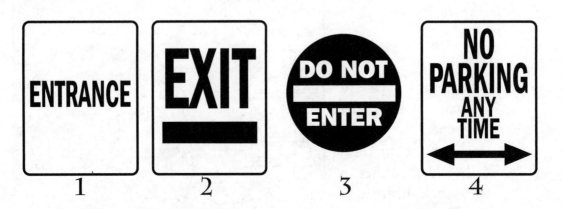

1   2   3   4

6 Which of these signs tells you that you can come in this door?

- ○ Sign 1
- ○ Sign 2
- ○ Sign 3
- ○ Sign 4

Selection 7

Read this weather chart. It shows what the weather will be like from Monday to Friday.

MONDAY	TUESDAY	WEDNESDAY	THURSDAY	FRIDAY
WARM AND SUNNY	WARM AND SUNNY	RAINY	CLOUDY	PARTLY CLOUDY

7 **Which day will NOT be good for playing outdoors?**

- ○ Tuesday
- ○ Wednesday
- ○ Thursday
- ○ Friday

Selection 8

Now read the next two stories and answer the question.

THE CROW AND THE PITCHER

It was very dry, and the birds were having trouble finding something to drink. A thirsty crow found a pitcher with a little water in the bottom of it. But the pitcher was too high and had a narrow neck. No matter how hard he tried, the crow could not reach into the pitcher far enough to get a drink of water. The poor thing felt as if he would die of thirst.

Then an idea came to him. Picking up some small stones, he dropped them into the pitcher one by one. With each stone the water rose a little higher until at last it was near enough so he could drink.

THE WOLF AND THE SHEEP

A wolf had been hurt in a fight with a bear. He was unable to move. He wasn't able to get to his food or to the stream to drink some water. A sheep passed by his hiding place. The wolf called to him.

"Please get me a drink of water," he begged. "The water would give me enough strength so I can get some solid food."

"Solid food!" said the sheep. "That means me, I suppose. If I brought you a drink, you would use it to wash me down your throat. Don't talk to me about a drink."

8 **How are these two passages alike?**

A They are both about a bear.

B They are both stories about animals.

C They are both unhappy stories.

D They are both true.

4 | LEARNING STUDY SKILLS

Suppose your teacher asks you to write a report about George Washington. You will need to find some information about his life.

In this chapter you will learn how to find information when you need it.

You will learn about different kinds of **reference books**. You will also find out how to use **tables of contents** and **indexes**.

USING REFERENCE BOOKS

Reference books are a good place to look for information. Here are the reference sources you will use most often:

- **Dictionaries** tell you what words mean and how to spell them.

- **Thesauruses** help you find synonyms (words that mean the same) and antonyms (words that mean the opposite) of words.

- **Encyclopedias** have information about many different topics. This information is arranged in alphabetical order.

- **Atlases** are books of maps. An atlas may have maps of the whole world or maps of just one area.

Computers can help you find a lot of information. Your home or library computer may have a dictionary, an encyclopedia, and even an atlas on CD-ROM. You may also find this information by going online and using the Internet.

Use the computer dictionary, encyclopedia, and atlas the same way you would a dictionary, encyclopedia, or atlas in a book.

Read Example 1 and decide which reference material would be most helpful.

Example 1

Boxing is a dangerous sport. Fighters often get cut lips and broken noses. Their heads may be badly hurt.

Boxing used to be even more dangerous than it is today. There were no rules at all. Fighters would punch each other until one of them couldn't fight any longer.

Finally, a man called the Marquess of Queensbury came up with some rules. They are called the Queensbury Rules. These rules made boxing safer. But it's still a very dangerous sport.

1A **Which reference source would be most likely to tell you what the Queensbury Rules say?**

    A   a dictionary

    B   an encyclopedia

    C   a thesaurus

    D   an atlas

The correct answer is B. You read that encyclopedias contain information about many topics. This includes sports.

1B The Marquess of Queensbury came from a country called Scotland. Which reference source would show you where Scotland is?

A a dictionary

B an encyclopedia

C a thesaurus

D an atlas

 Your teacher will discuss your answer.

Dictionaries

A dictionary lists words in alphabetical order. There are two **guidewords** at the top of each dictionary page. These guidewords will help you find the word you want to look up.

Suppose you want to look up the meaning of the word *origin*. You skim through the dictionary until you find these guidewords:

order • osprey

You know your alphabet. You know that *origin* comes after *order* and before *osprey*. So you know that you will find the word *origin* on the same page as these guidewords.

Example 2

 2 You want to look up the meaning of the word *cram*. Which dictionary guidewords tell you that you have found the page that has this word?

 A butter • cave

 B cow • crawl

 C cruel • curly

 D cute • dare

The correct answer is B. The word *cram* fits between the guidewords *cow* and *crawl*.

LOCATING INFORMATION IN BOOKS

Titles

The first thing you see about a book is its **title**. A title usually gives you a good sense of what a book is about.

Earlier in this chapter, we talked about writing a report on George Washington, our first president. Imagine that you are trying to find some information about him. You look at a shelf full of books. Which one would be most helpful?

Example 3

3   **In which book would you be most likely to find information about George Washington?**

A   American Presidents

B   The Animals and Plants of Indiana

C   Towns in Colonial Days

D   Native Americans

The correct answer is Choice A. George Washington was an American President. A book about American Presidents would tell you about him.

Table of Contents

Suppose you had to write about how birds fly. Your mother has a book at home about birds. How could you quickly decide if it would be helpful?

The answer is to look at the book's **table of contents**. A table of contents appears near the front of a book. It lists the names of the book's chapters and the page on which each chapter begins.

In Example 4, you can see part of the table of contents from a book about birds.

Example 4

TABLE OF CONTENTS

4   **Which chapter might be helpful if you wanted to learn how birds fly?**

   A   Chapter 1

   B   Chapter 2

   C   Chapter 4

   D   Chapter 5

Choice C is correct. Chapter 4 would probably tell you a good deal about how birds are able to fly.

Using an Index

A book's **index** is another good way to find information in a book. The index is at the back of a book.

Here is part of the index from another bird book:

> Backbone, *6*
>
> Bald eagle, *77* (photograph)
>
> Baltimore oriole, *99, 118*
>
> Barn owl, *55*
>
> Beak, *2, 4, 67-73, 71* (drawing)

An index is always in alphabetical order. It lists the topics, names, or places that are covered in the book. Then it tells you the pages on which they appear. For example, you can learn more about the barn owl if you turn to page 55.

Example 5

> Holly, *127-128*
>
> House wren, *95, 121, 128*
>
> How birds keep warm, *48-50*
>
> Hummingbirds, *22, 37-42, 68, 71, 78, 83, 99* (photograph)

5 You want to know how birds stay alive during a cold winter. Which would be the best pages to check?

  A pages 127-128

  B page 95 and 121

  C pages 48-50

  D pages 37-42

Choice C is correct. Pages 48-50 tell you how birds keep warm.

HELPFUL HINTS FOR IMPROVING YOUR RESEARCH SKILLS

1. Use **dictionaries** to find out what words mean. Remember that dictionaries are arranged in alphabetical order. A good way to find a word in a dictionary is to check the guidewords at the top of the page.

2. **Encyclopedias** contain all kinds of general information. They are arranged in alphabetical order.

3. **Atlases** will help you find places. They have many maps.

4. The **table of contents** is at the beginning of a book. The **index** is at the end. An index is in alphabetical order.

5. Book **titles** tell you what a book is about. Read them carefully.

6. Ask a teacher or librarian to help you find information using a computer. There are dictionaries, encyclopedias, and atlases on computers.

SELECTIONS FOR PRACTICE

Read each selection and answer the question or questions. Each answer choice has a bubble in front. Fill in the bubble next to the best choice.

Selection 1

Redwood trees are among the largest trees in the world. They are also among the oldest. They can live for hundreds of years. Two hundred years ago, northern California was filled with redwood trees. But people wanted to grow food where the redwoods stood. Many of these *giant* trees were cut down.

1A **If you wanted to see how far northern California is from Fort Wayne, where should you look?**

- O in a dictionary
- O in an encyclopedia
- O in a thesaurus
- O in an atlas

1B **Which of the following would be a good book to use if you wanted to find out the meaning of the word *giant*?**

- O a dictionary
- O an encyclopedia
- O a thesaurus
- O an atlas

Selection 2

2 **What kind of information would you be most likely to find in an encyclopedia?**

○   the meaning of the word *fanciful*

○   a street map of Indianapolis, Indiana

○   the names of the movies playing at your local movie theater

○   the main farm products of Indiana

Selection 3

3 **You want to look up the meaning of the word *wonder*. Which dictionary guidewords tell you that you have found the page that has this word?**

○   visit • wade

○   wand • weak

○   wipe • while

○   wolf • worry

Selection 4

4 **Which of the following would be a good book to use if you wanted to know more about Maria Tallchief, who was a great ballet dancer?**

○   Gifts Through the Ages

○   How Boxers Are Trained Today

○   Greatest Dancers of All Time

○   A History of Water Sports

Selection 5

TABLE OF CONTENTS

5 **Look at this table of contents. In what kind of book would these topics appear?**

○ a book about computers

○ a history book

○ a book about math

○ a book about spending your money wisely

Selection 6

> Aztec pyramids, *98-99*
>
> beaches, *19-23*
>
> bullfighting, *14, 47*
>
> Cinco de Mayo, *27, 54*
>
> fiestas, *101-104*
>
> Guadalajara, *89-91*
>
> Mexico City, *93-97*

6A Here is part of an index. What kind of book do you think it comes from?

- ○ a travel guide to Mexico
- ○ a book about animals
- ○ a book about dinosaurs
- ○ a book about how to find a good doctor

6B Suppose you were looking for places to swim. Which pages might help you?

- ○ 19-23
- ○ 14 and 47
- ○ 98-99
- ○ 101-104

PART 2: COMPREHENSION STRATEGIES

5 | READING FOR FACTS

Often the answer to a question is right there in the story. Suppose you read a story about pigs. The story says: "Pigs are really very clean animals." Then the question asks if pigs are pretty or clean or fat. You have just read that pigs are clean, so you check "clean." The correct answer was in the story.

Read this example and answer the question.

Example 1

We didn't like Shana's birthday party. The music was boring. The pizza was the worst pizza we ever had. The cake was okay, but the pieces were too small. After we ate, we played games. They were really dopey. The only thing that was really good was the popcorn. It was colored red, blue, and green. We ate a huge amount. It tasted just great.

1 **What did we like at Shana's party?**

   A   the games

   B   the pizza

   C   the music

   D   the popcorn

To find the right answer, you have to read all the choices. Then you have to read the selection again to find the choice that is right. The correct choice is D, *the popcorn*. The answer is right there in the selection. If you look back in the selection, you can be sure to get it right.

Read Example 2. Look back in the selection to be sure you've got the right answer.

Example 2

Blue Whale

The blue whale is the biggest animal in the world. It lives in the sea. It is usually 20 feet long when it is born. The adult can grow to almost 110 feet long.

2 **How big is the baby blue whale?**

    A   12 feet

    B   13 feet

    C   20 feet

    D   110 feet

Look back to find the answer. Check each choice against the information in the story. Read all the choices before you pick an answer.

 Your teacher will discuss your answer.

HELPFUL HINTS FOR READING FOR FACTS

1. Find the part of the story that has the facts you need to answer the question.

2. Read this part of the selection again. Check each choice to find the one that fits the facts in the story.

3. Remember to read all the choices. Decide which choice is most like what you have read. Pick the best answer.

SELECTIONS FOR PRACTICE

Selection 1

Mr. Waters started to work at six in the morning. He ate nothing until ten o'clock. Then he sat down to eat a big breakfast. He liked to start with four pancakes. He always had two or three eggs with toast. Sometimes when he was still hungry, he ate four or five slices of bacon. He finished the meal with a cup of hot chocolate.

1 **How did Mr. Waters eat?**

O He ate breakfast at 6 A.M.

O He began his breakfast with pancakes.

O He had five eggs with bacon for breakfast.

O He drank hot chocolate before he had breakfast.

Selection 2

People sleep lying down. Most animals sleep lying down, too. That's the way lions and wolves sleep. But some animals, like the giraffe, sleep standing up. A few water birds sleep standing on just one leg. Bats sleep in a really odd way. They hang upside down when they sleep.

2 **How do most animals sleep?**

O   They stand up.

O   Bats keep flying when they sleep.

O   They sleep upside down.

O   They sleep lying down.

Selection 3

A diamond in a ring is a very special kind of stone. It sparkles and shines. It is worth a lot of money. But most diamonds aren't like this. They aren't large or beautiful or worth a lot of money. They are small. They don't shine. But they are still very useful. Diamonds are the hardest things on earth. So these small diamonds are used to cut and grind very hard metal.

3 **Most diamonds are**

O   small

O   used in rings

O   shiny

O   worth a lot of money

6 | MAKING INFERENCES

Some questions are about facts in the story. But most questions are not. You must figure them out for yourself. You must use your head.

Suppose you read a story about cats. The story says: "Cats wash themselves all the time."

Then the question asks you about cats. It asks you if cats are dirty, or clean, or smelly.

The story doesn't have the words: "Cats are clean." But it does say they wash themselves all the time. You can figure out the answer. Use your head. Cats wash themselves all the time, so they must be clean. When you figure out an answer to a question by using your head, this is called **making an inference**.

The next example has this kind of question.

Example 1

Fred was playing with his cousin Jeff. They were up in a tree, working on a tree house. Then Jeff stepped onto a dead branch. Fred heard a crack and a sudden cry. A moment later he heard a thump from below.

Fred knew without looking around what had happened.

1   **What happened?**

   A   Fred and his cousin had a fight.

   B   Jeff had finished the tree house.

   C   Jeff fell out of the tree.

   D   Fred had an accident.

The answer is NOT in the story. But you can make a smart guess about the right answer. You read that both boys were up in a tree. Then you read that Jeff stepped onto a dead branch. When Fred hears a crack, a cry, and a thump on the ground, you can guess that the branch broke and Jeff fell to the ground. So you can figure out that C is PROBABLY the correct answer.

Now read the next example. See if you can make a good guess about the correct answer.

Example 2

Miranda is nine today, and she is very excited. She knows she will have a birthday party, and she knows her mother is buying her a gift. She hopes it's not a dress. Her mother always buys silly dresses for her. She can't guess what her gift will be.

When she gets home, Miranda hears a very strange sound. Then she sees a small tail wagging behind the door. Now she knows what her gift is. She is very, very happy.

2 **Why is Miranda happy?**

    A   because her mother gave her a dress

    B   because her birthday present is a puppy

    C   because she is home

    D   because she's going to the zoo

The story gives you clues about what Miranda got for her birthday. You can guess from the strange sound and the wagging tail that she got a puppy. That is why she is happy. Choice B is the correct answer.

HELPFUL HINTS
FOR MAKING INFERENCES

1. Remember that the answer may not be stated in the story. You may need to figure out the answer to some questions.

2. Use clues in the story to figure out the best answer. Then add what you know about the event or topic. These two steps will help you to make good **inferences** or guesses.

SELECTIONS FOR PRACTICE

You won't find the answers to these questions written in the story. But you will find clues that will help you. Use the clues and what you know to figure out the answers.

Selection 1

Mindy had a spelling test today. Mindy looked very sleepy as she rode on the school bus. She looked like she was thinking about something very important. Just before the test, Mindy looked worried. After the test, Mindy was smiling.

1 **Why was Mindy smiling after the test?**

O   She felt that she did well on the test.

O   She was still worried.

O   She was going home.

O   She did not care about the test.

Selection 2

Jack has been my best friend since we were six. Two years ago, his family moved into our building. He lives one floor above me. Now we do our homework together and hang out almost every day.

2 **How does the speaker feel about having Jack in his building?**

O He is very happy about it.

O He can't make up his mind about it.

O He doesn't like it.

O He wants to do his homework alone.

Selection 3

During the first month of basketball, Shawna couldn't score very many points. The ball went too high or too far to the left. She only made two baskets in ten shots.

But she kept at it. By the end of the third month, she was getting six out of ten shots in the basket. All the work she put in really paid off.

3   **Why did Shawna play better in the third month?**

     O   Shawna grew five inches.

     O   Shawna got new sneakers.

     O   Shawna made a lot of friends.

     O   Shawna practiced a lot.

Selection 4

Mr. Medina gave his son Luis his birthday present. Luis shook it. Nothing rattled. He smelled it. Nothing smelled.

Slowly, Luis began to unwrap his gift. When he took off the paper, he found a white box. When he took the lid off the box, he found more paper. Luis tore the paper away. Finally he could see his gift.

His father had given him a pair of sneakers. There was nothing else in the whole world he wanted more. For weeks he had given his father hints. He said his old sneakers were worn out. He said his friend Jimmy had a new pair of sneakers. But his father didn't seem to listen. He just kept working on his car or whatever else he was doing.

But Mr. Medina had heard after all!

4   **How did Mr. Medina show he was listening to Luis?**

     O   He forgot Luis's birthday.

     O   He bought Luis what he wanted.

     O   He tried to fix his car.

     O   He talked about Luis's friend Jimmy.

7 IDENTIFYING CAUSES AND EFFECTS

When reading a story, it is often useful to know *why* something happened. The reason why something happens in a story is called the **cause**. The event or action that happens as a result of the cause is called the **effect**.

Sometimes writers use the word *because* to help us understand why something happened.

Read the next selection and decide why Tobie is one of Mr. Peterson's favorite pets. Watch out for the word *because*.

Example 1

Tobie wasn't a loving cat. He didn't like to be petted. He hissed at strangers, and sometimes he scratched the furniture. He had bad habits. Even so, Tobie was Mr. Peterson's favorite pet. This was because he was a great hunter and he kept mice out of the cellar.

1 **Tobie was Mr. Peterson's favorite pet because**

    A   he was a good hunter

    B   he didn't like to be petted

    C   he jumped on people

    D   he scratched the furniture

The correct answer is A.

Some passages explain why things happen without using key words like *because*. See if you can figure out the answer in Example 2.

Example 2

Weightlifting

José, Leroy, and Sanjae all took up weightlifting. At first they worked out for a half hour every Monday, Wednesday, and Friday. But now that they've been doing it for a few months, they work out for an hour every day. One thing they all notice is that their clothes feel very tight. They all need to wear bigger shirts.

2 **Why don't clothes fit José, Leroy, and Sanjae anymore?**

A   The company that makes their clothes makes bad shirts.

B   They are getting sick from lifting weights.

C   They now have bigger chests and more muscles.

D   The clothes shrank in the dryer.

Your teacher will discuss your answer.

HELPFUL HINTS
FOR IDENTIFYING CAUSES AND EFFECTS

1. Watch out for key words that tell you about **cause** and **effect**.

The words that follow the key word explain what caused something or what its effect was.

2. When there are no key words, ask yourself why an event happened—its cause. The answer will be there in the passage.

SELECTIONS FOR PRACTICE

Selection 1

Eugene carried his groceries to his car in a paper bag. The bottom of the bag felt wet. He put the bag in the car and drove home. When he picked it up to take into his house, the bottom of the bag tore open. All the groceries fell out. The milk carton broke and all the milk leaked out.

1 **The groceries fell out because**

O   the bag was wet

O   the bag was in the car

O   the bag was made of paper

O   the milk carton was cold

Selection 2

Peach was having a party. She invited all her friends to come. Her mother made sandwiches and popcorn. That afternoon Peach baked a chocolate cake for her friends. It looked nice and smelled delicious. She took a bite to see how it tasted. It was very good. She had one more slice. It was the best chocolate cake she had ever made. She ate another slice. Then she ate another. When her friends arrived, they had sandwiches and popcorn. But there wasn't any chocolate cake left.

2 **Why wasn't there any chocolate cake left?**

    O   Peach ate it.

    O   Peach gave it to her mother.

    O   Peach put it in the refrigerator.

    O   Peach threw it away.

Selection 3

Ella and Jack invited us to supper. They had just been married and were both learning to cook. The food tasted terrible. The fish was burned. The potatoes were not completely cooked. After the meal, we decided we would never eat at their house again.

Three weeks later, Ella and Jack invited us to supper again. We didn't want to go. But we didn't want to hurt their feelings. Ella and Jack are our friends, even if they are poor cooks.

We had an idea. We called and said we'd love to come and we'd like to bring Chinese food with us. They were a bit surprised, but they agreed. We bought the food at a take-out place, and everyone enjoyed the meal.

3 **Ella and Jack were surprised because**

O   they didn't like Chinese food

O   we called

O   we wanted to bring Chinese food

O   they are our friends

8 | FACT AND OPINION

Sometimes we need to tell if a statement is **fact** or **opinion**. (Another name for opinion is non-fact.)

Here are some facts and some opinions.

FACTS	OPINIONS
Herb has black hair.	Herb has a cute nose.
Washington was our first president.	Washington was our best president.
Jackie went to the movies at noon.	Jackie should be a model.

A **fact** is something you can check. You can find out if it is true.

An **opinion** is based on feelings. Even if it's a good opinion, it can't be proved.

Write **F** if it's a fact.

Write **O** if it's an opinion.

_____ Lincoln was a great president.

_____ Neil is 6 feet tall.

_____ Alan weighs 295 lbs.

- "Lincoln was a great President" is an opinion. Some people may not think he was a great president.

- The other two statements, that Neil is 6 feet tall and that Alan weighs 295 lbs., are facts. They can be checked and proven.

Read Example 1. Decide which sentence is fact and which sentences are fiction.

Example 1

(1) Philip looks clumsy when he plays baseball. (2) He'll never be any good at track. (3) He shouldn't even try to play basketball. (4) But he can lift 300 pounds.

1 **Which sentence contains a *fact*?**

   A   Sentence 1

   B   Sentence 2

   C   Sentence 3

   D   Sentence 4

The correct answer is D. The only fact is that Philip can lift 300 pounds. All the other statements are the author's opinions.

Example 2

A gold record is a record that sold more than half a million copies. Few singers have ever had a gold record. Elvis Presley had 21. He had more gold records than any other singer. He also made many movies. He is the greatest singer who ever lived.

2 **Which statement is an opinion?**

   A   Elvis Presley had 21 gold records.

   B   He is the greatest singer who ever lived.

   C   He made more gold records than anyone else.

   D   He made many movies.

The correct answer is B. This answer is based on feeling. The person who wrote this might think it's right. It might even be right. But it's not a fact. It can't be checked. All the other choices can be checked. They are facts.

HELPFUL HINTS FOR DISTINGUISHING BETWEEN FACT AND OPINION

1. Can you prove it? If so, it's a **fact**.
2. Does a statement show a person's feelings about a subject? If so, it is an **opinion**.

SELECTIONS FOR PRACTICE

Selection 1

There is a new car outside. It belongs to Karen. It is green with white trim. It is the prettiest car I've ever seen. Her mother bought it for her for her birthday.

1 **Which statement is an *opinion*?**

O   The car is a birthday present.

O   The car is green.

O   The car is new.

O   The car is pretty.

Selection 2

We make lots of foods from milk. Cream is made from milk. So is butter. So is ice cream. Cheese is also made from milk. Cheese tastes really good.

2 **Which is an *opinion*?**

- O   Cheese comes from milk.
- O   Cheese tastes good.
- O   Many foods are made from milk.
- O   Ice cream comes from milk.

Selection 3

The Great Train Robbery was made in 1903. It was the first Western movie ever made. It had gunfights, fist fights on top of a moving train, and gangsters attacking a town on fast horses. It was only nine minutes long, but it was very popular. There were long lines to see it when it first opened. I saw it for the first time last week. The audience clapped for five minutes when it ended. It was the first Western and it is still the most exciting Western ever made. In fact, it's one of the greatest movies of all time.

3 **Which statement is an *opinion*?**

- O   *The Great Train Robbery* was nine minutes long.
- O   *The Great Train Robbery* was made in 1903.
- O   *The Great Train Robbery* is exciting.
- O   *The Great Train Robbery* was the first Western movie ever made.

PART 3: READING COMPREHENSION AND LITERATURE

Long before there were any books, people told stories. Other people listened and remembered them. They then told these stories to their children. After thousands of years, people began to write their stories down.

Every story has one or more **characters**. Usually they are people, but they could be animals. Every story has a **setting**. The setting is when and where the story takes place. Every story has a **plot**—something happens.

Most of the stories from very long ago were told as poems. Today, most stories are not poems. But poets still write poems, and people enjoy reading them.

In Part 3, you will learn about different kinds of stories and poems. You will learn ways to understand and enjoy them.

9 | IDENTIFYING DETAILS THAT DESCRIBE CHARACTERS IN A STORY

Stories are usually about people. The people in a story are called **characters**. The author describes the characters by telling you details about them. Details that describe characters may include the information that a character is happy or maybe sad. Other details may tell you that a character is funny or angry. These details tell you about a **character's feelings**.

See if you can tell how Juana feels in this example.

Example 1

Juana's sister took her to a movie. It was the story of a clown. When the clown did his tricks, Juana started to laugh. She told her sister it was the funniest movie she had ever seen.

1 **The movie made Juana feel**

    A sad

    B hungry

    C happy

    D sick

The correct choice is C. The selection tells us that the movie made Juana laugh. It made her happy.

Some authors use words like *brave*, *lazy*, or *strong* to describe their characters. Other authors make you figure out what their characters are like from what they do.

Read the next example and figure out how to describe Carlos.

Example 2

Carlos knew that bears were near. He couldn't see them, but he could hear them moving in the woods. He quickly built several fires around his tent. He kept the fires going all night. In the morning, the bears were gone.

2 **How would you describe Carlos?**

A very lazy

B confused

C smart

D stupid

The correct choice is C, *smart*. The author tells us that Carlos could hear the bears in the woods. He knows they are dangerous. He builds fires and keeps them going all night. Carlos was smart to figure out that fires would keep the bears away. All the other choices are wrong.

COMPARING CHARACTERS

In some stories there are two or more characters. You may be asked to compare them. You do this by trying to decide how they are alike and how they are different.

Example 3

Hank just does not care about baseball. When his brother Fred watches baseball on TV, Hank reads a comic. Hank thinks football is exciting. He's happy to watch tennis. He likes every sport but baseball.

3 **How are Hank and Fred different?**

   A   Fred likes football best, and Hank likes baseball best.

   B   Fred likes sports, but Hank does not.

   C   Hank likes sports, but Fred does not.

   D   Hank does not like baseball, but Fred does.

The correct answer is D, *Hank does not like baseball, but Fred does.* You read that Hank reads a comic whenever Fred watches baseball on TV. You also read that Hank likes all sports except baseball. This tells you that the other choices are wrong.

Example 4

Jesse was 6 foot 2 and tough as iron. But he had hardly ever been in the woods. His sister Melody loved the woods. One Saturday, Jesse took a walk in the woods with his sister. He heard a lot of strange sounds. He heard one sound that seemed very close. Jesse looked worried. He was afraid of snakes. But Melody showed him where to look. She pointed to where a small bird was hopping in the leaves. Jesse laughed. Then he felt better.

4 **How is Melody different from Jesse?**

A She is taller.

B She is stronger.

C She knows more about the woods.

D She is better in reading and writing.

 Your teacher will discuss your answer.

HELPFUL HINTS FOR IDENTIFYING DETAILS THAT DESCRIBE CHARACTERS

1. A **character** is a person in the story. Look for details that tell you how the character acts and feels.

2. Decide what word or words describe the character.

3. Sometimes there are two characters in the story. Decide how they are alike and how they are different.

SELECTIONS FOR PRACTICE

Selection 1

Carl got married last Saturday. He married Alicia, whom he has known since kindergarten. Carl got lost on the way to the church. And he forgot the wedding ring. His sister Angie gave Carl her ring. Carl used it for the wedding. Later he found the missing ring. It was in his pocket all the time.

1   **How was Carl feeling on his wedding day?**

- ○   calm
- ○   nervous
- ○   sick
- ○   wonderful

Selection 2

Larry's bed was not made. His toys were on the floor. So were his clothes. He had eaten an ice cream cone a few days ago. You could tell because there were chocolate colored drips on his rug that led from the door to his bed.

He hadn't combed his hair when he left for school that morning. There were spots on his shirt. Larry's shoes were not tied. You could see yellow bits of the egg he had for breakfast on his face. He had worked on his bike yesterday. You could tell from the black under his fingernails.

2   **Which words best describe Larry?**

- ○   hungry and rushed
- ○   sloppy and careless
- ○   sleepy and sad
- ○   nice and kind

Selection 3

Nora opened every box that she saw. If there was a hole in the ground, Nora poked it with a stick. If there was a closed door, she peeked in. No one could keep a secret from her. She wanted to know why the sky is blue. She wanted to know how bees make honey. She wanted to know how old everyone was. Once her family tried to have a surprise birthday party for her, but she couldn't be surprised. She never missed a thing. She caught her mother whispering the secret when no one knew she was there. Nora wanted to know everything about everything and she usually did.

3 **A good word to describe Nora would be**

- O   curious
- O   worried
- O   shy
- O   smart

Selection 4

Sara and Brittany played together every day. They liked to play school. Brittany usually played the teacher, and Sara usually pretended to be her student. Brittany told Sara what to do. She gave her math problems. She asked her to read out loud. It was fun for both of them.

One day Sara tried to be the teacher. She found that she didn't like being in charge. She had a hard time, so she asked Brittany for ideas. She just didn't know what to tell Brittany to do. Although they still took turns, they decided it was much easier for Brittany to be the teacher.

pretend =
make believe

4 **How is Brittany different from Sara?**

- O   She is a better leader than Sara.
- O   She is better at math and reading than Sara.
- O   She is a lot older than Sara.
- O   She has more fun than Sara.

Selection 5

Daniel was always laughing. He knew how to have a good time. His laughter was catching. Everyone around him was soon laughing, too. Daniel had lots of good friends. He liked people and people liked him. His brother Andy didn't laugh much. He had nothing against other people. It's just that he preferred to be alone, reading or making things. Both boys were happy being who they were.

5 **How were Daniel and Andy different?**

○ Andy liked to laugh and have fun.

○ Daniel liked to read and make things.

○ Andy liked people more.

○ Daniel liked to laugh more.

10 IDENTIFYING DETAILS THAT DESCRIBE SETTINGS

A story's **setting** tells you *where* and *when* the story takes place. Sometimes the author will name the setting. Sometimes you must identify the setting yourself.

Read the next story and decide where it takes place.

> Billy took a deep breath and jumped in the water. The hot sun had made the water quite warm. Billy swam to the other side and climbed out.

You know Billy is swimming somewhere. It probably isn't the ocean. You can't swim to the other side of the ocean. You can guess that Billy is at a swimming pool or a lake. You can also guess that it is summer because the sun is hot.

These three sentences about Billy tell you *where* the story is probably set—in a lake or swimming pool. They also tell *when* the story is set—during the summer. The author didn't tell you this. You worked it out for yourself.

A story may take place in a swimming pool, or in a submarine under the ocean, or in the streets of a modern city. The "Star Trek" stories are set in a spaceship in the distant future.

Read the next example. Decide where this story is set.

Example 1

Jordan looked around the store. A teddy bear sat on a chair. A little train went around in a big circle. A big doll with blue eyes sat drinking tea with her friends. There were lots of stuffed animals, too. Jordan picked up a small stuffed cat and felt its fur. It was very soft. It was bright yellow and had pointy ears.

1   **Where does this story take place?**

   A   in a railroad yard

   B   in a restaurant

   C   in a zoo

   D   in a toy store

The story says that Jordan is in a store. You can tell that it is a toy store by the toys he sees. Choice D is the correct answer.

Read Example 2 and decide when this story takes place.

Example 2

It was getting warm, too warm to wear a heavy jacket. The snow had melted. The grass was starting to turn a bright shade of green. The sun was getting higher in the sky. Soon they would be able to spend the entire day outdoors. Leroy looked forward to it every year. It was a time of hope.

2   **This selection probably takes place**

   A   in the spring

   B   in the summer

   C   in the fall

   D   in the winter

The correct answer is A. The winter snow has just melted and the grass is getting greener. These things happen in the spring.

A story can take place in winter or summer. It may be set 1,000 years ago, or today, or next week. It may be set in the morning or at night.

Read Example 3 and decide when it takes place.

Example 3

Most of the buildings were dark. Some still had lights on, but only in a few rooms. There were very few cars still on the road, and their headlights lit up the whole street. The city was quiet.

3 **What time was it?**

    A   about 9 A.M.

    B   about 12 noon

    C   about 3 in the afternoon

    D   late at night

 Your teacher will discuss your answer.

COMPARING SETTINGS

In many stories, the setting changes from one place to another. People travel from home to work. They visit their friends. They go to the movies. They go to school and to worship.

Different settings can play an important part in a story.

Example 4

At six o'clock, the sky grew dark and it began to rain. It was still raining an hour later when Keisha went to visit her aunt. Aunt Lina was lying in bed and a nurse was speaking to her. When the nurse left, Keisha kissed her aunt's pale cheek. She was upset to find her looking so ill. Aunt Lina laughed at Keisha's long, sad face.

"Don't worry," she said. "I'm not as sick as I look. The doctor says I'll be up and about soon."

Two weeks later, Keisha was doing her homework. Through the window she could see the sun shining and the leaves blowing in the breeze. There came a knock at the door and she ran to open it. There stood Aunt Lina carrying a big bunch of flowers.

"You came to see me," she said, "so now I'm here to visit you."

4A **We can guess that this selection begins in**

A a hospital

B a hotel

C Keisha's home

D a beauty parlor

The correct answer is A. You know it is a hospital because Aunt Lina is in bed and a nurse is speaking to her.

NOTICE: Photocopying any part of this book is forbidden by law.

4B   **Where is Keisha at the end of this story?**

  A   at Aunt Lina's home

  B   at home

  C   at the hospital

  D   at school

 Your teacher will discuss your answer.

HELPFUL HINTS FOR IDENTIFYING DETAILS THAT DESCRIBE A STORY'S SETTING

1. Look for clues to help you figure out **where** the story takes place. Your own experiences and what you know about the world will help you.

2. Look for clues that tell you **when** the story takes place. Is it before or after something? Are there clues that tell you the time of day, or the time of the year, or a time in the past or future?

SELECTIONS FOR PRACTICE

Read the following selections and decide on their settings.

Selection 1

We took the elevator to the 40th floor. We went outside and looked down at the city streets. We could see people crossing the road. They looked just like ants.

1 **Where is this story set?**

O   in a skyscraper

O   in a zoo

O   on a ship

O   on a plane

Selection 2

Mark and Jeff had an ant farm in their classroom. They decided they wanted to have one at home as well.

Jeff said, "We'll get a tank and some sand. We can put the ants in the tank. They'll dig their homes in the sand, and then we'll have our own ant farm."

So Mark and Jeff went out to find some ants. They started to dig for ants in a farmer's field. It was very hard work. There was a lot of ice on the ground. The mud was frozen.

They dug and dug, but they did not find one ant! They were getting very cold and hungry. They were ready for lunch. Finally, they went home empty-handed.

2A   **Where would you guess Mark and Jeff live?**

- O   in the city
- O   in the country
- O   in the mountains
- O   near the ocean

2B   **This story takes place**

- O   at night in the spring
- O   in late morning in the summer
- O   in the evening in the fall
- O   in the afternoon in the winter

Selection 3

Poor Cinderella! She wanted to go to the ball. Her sisters were going. All day long she watched them get ready. But Cinderella couldn't go. She had no dress to wear to a dance. And besides, her older sisters said she had to stay home and clean the house.

At 7 P.M., her sisters left for the ball. Then Cinderella began to clean the large, chilly house. It took her a long time. There were so many rooms.

Cinderella started cleaning in the attic. Then she worked her way downstairs. She dusted all the furniture. She made all the beds. She swept the floors. Finally, she washed all the dishes in the kitchen sink.

By the time she finished cleaning, it was after eleven o'clock. She was very tired. A small tear came out of the corner of her eye.

She wondered what it would be like to be at the ball. She imagined a big, old castle with huge rooms and high ceilings. She could see the fireplace and the roaring fire that kept everyone warm. She imagined the large, glowing lamps, the happy faces, and the beautiful ball gowns.

But alas, she would never go there. She would never know.

3A **How much time passes during this story?**

- O   one hour
- O   a few hours
- O   a day
- O   a week

3B **What kind of home does Cinderella live in?**

- O   a big, old house
- O   a mobile home
- O   a small cottage in the country
- O   a modern apartment

3C **Cinderella thought the castle was different from her home. How was it different?**

- O   The castle was cold and lonely.
- O   The castle was smaller.
- O   The castle was warmer and more cheerful.
- O   The castle and the house were both very small.

11 STORY PLOT, STORY PROBLEMS, AND SEQUENCE

Stories are about things that happen. The things that happen in a story are called the **plot**. The plot is made up of the important things that happen to the main character in the story.

Read this story. What is the most important thing to happen to Louisa in this story?

Example 1

Louisa got up a little late on Tuesday morning. Then she played with her doll for ten minutes. She took a long time to eat her breakfast. When she left the house, she saw the school bus. It was driving away without her. Louisa came to school really late that day.

1   **What was the most important thing to happen to Louisa in this story?**

    A   Louisa ate breakfast.

    B   Louisa played with her dolls.

    C   Louisa missed the bus.

    D   Louisa left the house.

The answer is C. The most important thing to happen to Louisa was that she missed the bus. All the other events happened, but they were not the most important part of the story. Now read the following story and find the most important event.

Example 2

Muffin was Bobby's parrot. He loved to eat crackers. He could say Bobby's name. One day Bobby left the cage door open. Muffin got out. He flew through the door, and he was gone. We couldn't find him for three hours. Then, suddenly he flew back through the window. No one knows where he went. We were happy he came back.

Parrot

2 **What was the most important thing to happen in this story?**

A   Muffin ate crackers.

B   Muffin got out and came back.

C   Muffin said Bobby's name.

D   We couldn't find Muffin for three hours.

Choice B, Muffin got out of his cage, was the most important event.

HOW PROBLEMS GET SOLVED

Readers like to read a story that has a **central problem**. We like to read to find out how the problem gets solved.

The problem in the next paragraph is that Casey doesn't talk.

Casey wouldn't talk. She didn't say a word all through second grade. She would smile at her teachers. She would play with the other kids. But she never talked.

This story is interesting because we wonder what will happen to Casey.

Many stories have a plot with a problem that gets solved at the end. When the main problem is solved, this is called a **resolution**. Read how the problem with Casey gets solved.

Casey was silent all through second grade. But third grade was different. Casey got to be best friends with two other girls. She played and laughed with them all the time. And one day she said, "Hi." Then she began to talk some more. Now she won't stop talking.

The central problem in this story is that Casey wouldn't talk. The problem ended when Casey got to be friends with two other girls and started to talk. This is how the problem came to a resolution.

Here is another example of a story with a problem that gets solved.

Example 3

Jewel likes to read. She also likes it to be quiet when she does her homework. But her brother Hamid likes TV. He used to watch it all the time. And he kept it very loud.

Jewel would get really angry. She'd shout at her brother. But he wouldn't turn the TV off. And Jewel couldn't read because it was too noisy.

Then Hamid joined the basketball team. He practiced all the time. It is very quiet in Jewel's house now. She can read all she wants to. But she misses Hamid. She wishes he spent more time at home.

3A **What is the central problem in this story?**

    A Hamid and Jewel argue about which TV program to watch.

    B Hamid is angry because Jewel won't watch TV.

    C Jewel finds the TV too noisy.

    D Hamid doesn't read or do his homework.

The correct answer is C. Jewel wanted the house to be quiet. Hamid wanted to have the TV set on.

3B **How is this problem solved?**

A   Hamid joins a basketball team.

B   Hamid starts spending more time on his studies.

C   Jewel does her homework at her friend's house.

D   Jewel gives up on doing her homework.

 Your teacher will discuss your answer.

IDENTIFYING SEQUENCE OF EVENTS

A story often tells the order in which things happen. Words like *before* and *after*, or *first* and *last*, tell you the order, or sequence, in which things happen.

Read the next example. Decide when people stopped sitting near Amanda.

Example 4

Everyone liked Amanda when she first came to school. Even after she had a fight with Nancy, we still liked her. But after she started shooting rubber bands at everyone, she became a big pest. Now no one sits near her. Even her cousin Tommy doesn't want to be her friend anymore.

4 **Everyone stopped sitting near Amanda**

A   after she first came to school

B   after she hit Nancy

C   after she started shooting rubber bands

D   after Tommy stopped being friendly with her

The correct answer is C, *after she started shooting rubber bands*.

Sometimes you are asked for the order of events. But you don't have words like *before* and *after* to help you.

Here's one thing you can do. Find the story event that is mentioned in the question. Read the sentences *before* this event if you're asked what happened earlier. Read the sentences *after* this event if you're asked what happened later. This will usually give you the answer.

Read the next passage. Decide what happens before Donny hears the kitten's cry.

Example 5

Donny walked up the stairs and entered the large room. Suddenly he heard a small "mew." He looked inside the closets. They were empty. Still, he could hear a faint cry. He kept searching. Finally he found a kitten. It was hiding under a table. He lifted the kitten in his arms and carried it out of the house.

5　**What happened before Donny heard the kitten mewing?**

    A　He looked in the closets.

    B　He looked under the table.

    C　He lifted the kitten in his arms.

    D　He entered the room.

Choice D is correct. In the second sentence, Donny hears a kitten mew. In the sentence before that, you read that he entered the room.

HELPFUL HINTS
FOR STORY PROBLEMS, RESOLUTIONS,
AND SEQUENCE OF EVENTS

1. Try to find the **main problem** in a story. Try to find the event that caused this problem.

2. Notice how the story ends. Many stories end by solving their main problems.

3. If you must decide the order in which things happen, look for order words, such as *first*, *last*, *before*, and *after*.

4. If there are no order words, read the sentences before or after the event described in the question.

SELECTIONS FOR PRACTICE

Read the following selections and figure out what kind of problems the authors are describing. Then see how it is solved.

Selection 1

Jackie loved her snake, Sam. But it's hard having a snake for a pet. Some people are afraid of snakes. Jackie's mother wasn't afraid, but she didn't really like having a snake in the house. Jackie loved her pet, but she wanted her mother to be happy, too.

So Jackie spoke to Mr. Morris. He said he would keep Sam in the school zoo. So Jackie gave Sam to Mr. Morris. Jackie was sad, but she was pleased that other kids could see what a great pet Sam was.

She knew Mom would be happy Sam was gone. And Mr. Morris would feed Sam and keep his cage clean.

1A   **What is Jackie's problem?**

O   She is afraid of snakes.

O   Her mother doesn't like her having a pet snake.

O   She wants to give her snake to Mr. Morris.

O   Her mother is afraid of snakes.

1B   **Which event solves Jackie's problem?**

O   Her mom says she can keep Sam.

O   Mr. Morris agrees to keep Sam in the school zoo.

O   Mr. Morris cleans out Sam's cage.

O   The other kids see Sam in the school zoo.

Selection 2

Every day, Jessica and her younger brother, Jamal, went to school on the school bus. Usually the bus picked them up at 8:15 sharp. But last Friday, the bus was late. Jessica and Jamal were still waiting at 8:30.

Jessica thought they should walk. It should take them only half an hour to reach the school. Jamal didn't like that idea. He was wearing his new jeans. He didn't want to mess them up walking the dirty streets.

In the end, Jessica said she would walk to school by herself. Jamal wasn't happy, but he agreed to walk, too. The children were an hour late for school.

2A **What event caused a problem for Jessica and Jamal?**

O   Jamal and Jessica had a fight.

O   The school bus didn't come.

O   Jamal and Jessica were late and missed the bus.

O   Jamal and Jessica didn't want to take the school bus.

2B **How did the children solve their problem?**

O   They rode the bus.

O   They waited until 8:30.

O   They stayed home.

O   They walked to school.

2C **Why was Jamal unhappy with their solution?**

O   He didn't want to be late.

O   He didn't want to get his new jeans dirty.

O   He didn't want to go to school.

O   He didn't want to walk with his sister.

Selection 3

Floyd wanted to teach his little sister Lucy to read. He thought he'd start by reading to her as much as he could. He wanted to get her interested in reading. Then he taught Lucy the alphabet. It wasn't hard because they made a game of it. Next he taught her the beginning sound of each letter. They began practicing with little cards with easy words written on them. Then Floyd got some easy books with words Lucy knew. Pretty soon Lucy was reading to Floyd, instead of Floyd reading to Lucy.

3A **What was the first thing that Floyd did to teach his sister to read?**

- He taught her the beginning sounds of the letters.
- He read to her a lot.
- He taught her the alphabet.
- He got her easy books to read.

3B **What did Floyd do next after he taught Lucy the alphabet?**

- They practiced with little word cards.
- He taught her the beginning sounds.
- He read to her as much as possible.
- He tried to interest her in reading.

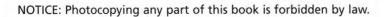

12 MAKING AND CONFIRMING PREDICTIONS BASED ON WHAT YOU READ

Flies like honey. Imagine that you have a jar of honey in a room full of flies. What do you think might happen?

You probably decided that the flies would come to the jar. You used what you read and what you know to decide what would happen next.

When you make a guess that something will happen, it is called **predicting** or **making a prediction**. As you read a story, you will often use your knowledge of the world around you and information from the story to **predict** what will happen next.

When your guess turns out to be right, that's called **confirming your prediction**.

See if you can predict what might happen next in this story.

Example 1

When Darlene is sick, her mother tells her to stay home from school. She stays in bed all day. This morning Darlene woke up with a very bad sore throat. Her head hurt her. She had a high fever.

1 **What will Darlene's mother *probably* say to Darlene?**

    A   Go out to play.

    B   Go to school.

    C   Stay in bed.

    D   Eat breakfast.

The best answer is C. Whenever Darlene is sick, her mother keeps her at home. Her mom will probably say, "Stay in bed."

Example 2

Marie got a bike for her birthday. At first she couldn't ride it. She kept falling down. But she kept trying. And now she rides everywhere.

Then Marie took some swimming lessons. At first she swam very badly.

2   **What do you think happened later?**

    A   She gave up swimming.

    B   She learned to swim well.

    C   She hated the water.

    D   She got sick.

 Your teacher will discuss your answer.

HELPFUL HINTS FOR MAKING AND CONFIRMING PREDICTIONS BASED ON WHAT YOU READ

1. When you are asked to **predict an outcome**, you must read the passage carefully. Make sure you understand what has happened so far.

2. Then you must make a good guess. You must guess what might happen based on what has happened so far.

3. You will not find the answer written in the passage. Choose the answer that makes the most sense.

SELECTIONS FOR PRACTICE

Selection 1

A chameleon is a strange kind of lizard. It can change the color of its skin. If it sits on a brown leaf, it looks brown. If it sits on a yellow leaf, its skin turns yellow.

1 **What do you suppose will happen if a chameleon sits on a green leaf?**

- ○ The leaf will turn brown.
- ○ The chameleon will move to a brown leaf.
- ○ Its skin will turn brown.
- ○ Its skin will turn green.

Selection 2

The Hawks are our high school basketball team. We like to watch them play. We cheer for them, and we are very happy when they win.

But lately, the Hawks have been playing badly. They miss their shots. They even drop the ball. Their coach shouts at them all the time. It makes them nervous. People say that a lot of Hawk players are unhappy.

2 **What will probably happen next time the Hawks play?**

- ○ They will beat the other team.
- ○ They will lose the game.
- ○ They will miss the game.
- ○ They will be the city champions.

Selection 3

Richard loved to play tricks on his brother Stuart. He loved to scare Stuart and watch him jump. Richard got home early one day and decided to have some fun with Stuart. He turned off all the lights in the house. Then he played a recording of some creepy sounds. He hid behind the door in Stuart's bedroom. Stuart walked into his room.

3 **What do you think might happen next?**

O   Stuart will take a nap.

O   Richard will say hello to Stuart.

O   Richard will jump out from behind the door.

O   Nothing will happen.

13 IDENTIFYING THE TOPIC OR THE MAIN IDEA

MAIN IDEA

The **topic** or **main idea** tells what happened in a passage. It is what the passage is mostly about.

There are many different ways to ask for the topic or main idea of a passage or story. Here are some:

- What is this story mostly about?

- What is the best title for the passage?

- Which idea is most important?

Sometimes the topic or main idea is right in the passage. Sometimes you have to figure out the main idea for yourself.

Read this selection. Then answer the question.

Example 1

The windows of this car are cracked. The lights won't go on. The motor needs a lot of work. The whole car is a piece of junk.

1 **What is the most important idea in this selection?**

A The car windows are cracked.

B The car motor needs work.

C The car is a piece of junk.

D The car lights don't work.

The correct choice is C, *the car is a piece of junk*. All the other choices are details that tell why the car is junk. The details tell why the main idea is true.

In Example 1, the main idea is stated right in the story. In Example 2, it is not. You have to use the details in the story to figure out the main idea.

Example 2

Ellen has two cats. She has a dog and a tank full of goldfish. She even has a bird named Tuffy and a lizard named Bud.

2 **The main idea is**

A   Ellen has a bird named Tuffy

B   Ellen has lots of pets

C   Ellen has two cats

D   Ellen likes fish

The correct choice is B, *Ellen has lots of pets*. This is the most important idea in the story. The selection says she likes fish, has cats and a dog, and that her bird is named Tuffy and her lizard is named Bud. But these are all details. You have to put the details together to get the main idea—Ellen has lots of pets.

THEME

A **theme** is something the story teaches you. It is a lesson you can use in life.

There are all sorts of possible story themes. A story theme might be something like:

Friends should be able to keep secrets.

Or it might be:

> New clothes can make you feel good.

Authors don't usually tell you what the theme is. You have to figure it out.

Example 3

Tania got a beautiful doll for her birthday. It cost a lot of money. She also got great new blades to skate with. And she got three new CD's. But she still didn't feel happy.

3 **What is the theme of this story?**

    A   Dolls cost too much.

    B   CD's make good gifts.

    C   Gifts alone don't make you happy.

    D   Tania likes to skate.

 Your teacher will discuss your answer.

HELPFUL HINTS FOR IDENTIFYING THE TOPIC, MAIN IDEA, AND THEME

1. Imagine you have just read a story. Someone asks you, "What was the story about?" Ask yourself how you could sum up the story in one sentence. This will help you decide on the **topic** or **main idea** of the story.

2. The **main idea** may be stated in the story. If it is not, you will have to use the details to figure out the topic or main idea, or what the story is mostly about.

3. A story **theme** is a lesson about life that the story teaches. The theme is usually not stated in the story. Most often you have to figure the theme out from the story.

4. Don't pick a theme that sounds good but isn't in the story.

SELECTIONS FOR PRACTICE

Selection 1

Dinosaurs came in all shapes and sizes. Some were as tall as a six-story building. Others were as small as a chicken. Some walked on four legs. Others walked on two. Some were hunters who ate other animals. Some ate only plants.

1 **What is the main idea?**

O   Dinosaurs ate other animals.

O   Some dinosaurs were small.

O   Some dinosaurs ate plants.

O   There were many different kinds of dinosaurs.

Selection 2

Most people think that the bottom of the ocean is very quiet. But now we know they are wrong. Scientists took listening machines down to the bottom of the sea. They heard a lot of whistles, beeps, and grunts. One scientist said it sounded like a traffic jam, with a lot of honking cars.

2 **The most important idea is that**

- O scientists didn't like the noises they heard
- O fish beep and whistle
- O there is a lot of noise under the sea
- O some scientists like to study the ocean

Selection 3

All the children love Mr. Zullo. He teaches them a lot, and they have fun in his class. He brings in animals. He loves to read stories. He acts and talks like the people in the stories. He can talk like a king or a little girl or an old woman. He tells the children to draw pictures of the people in his stories. He makes the class laugh by playing jokes. He sings a song at the end of the day. He is very special.

3 **What is this story mostly about?**

- O Children like to play with snakes and puppies.
- O It's fun to have a story read to you.
- O Mr. Zullo is a wonderful teacher.
- O Mr. Zullo plays lots of jokes.

Selection 4

The little ballet dancer on top of the music box was broken. One leg and arm had been chipped. But that didn't matter to Daisy. She thought it was the most beautiful music box she had ever seen. She touched the outside of the box. It felt very smooth. The box was gold and black and the light made it sparkle. Daisy opened it and the music started to play. It had a quiet, lovely sound. She smiled and started to dance.

4 **What is the theme of this story?**

O How something looks matters more than anything.

O It's fun to dance.

O Music is more important than anything.

O You can love something that isn't perfect.

14 | UNDERSTANDING POETRY

WHAT IS A POEM?

Often we can tell a **poem** just by looking at it. Each line is set off by itself. Each line usually begins with a capital letter.

Just like other authors, poets write for a certain reason. Sometimes they want to write about the world around them. Sometimes they want to tell how they feel about someone or something.

In this poem, the poet tells us how she thinks a daisy feels about life.

Example 1

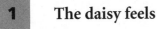

> I AM JUST A DAISY,
>
> NEITHER TALL NOR FAIR;
>
> BUT THE CHILDREN LOVE ME,
>
> SO WHY SHOULD I CARE?

1   **The daisy feels**

    A   happy that it is beautiful

    B   sad that it is not tall

    C   pleased that children love it

    D   surprised that no one cares about it

Choice C is the correct answer. The daisy doesn't think it is beautiful or tall, but it doesn't care. It is happy that children love it.

In Example 1, you had to figure out how a daisy feels. In the next poem, decide who or what makes the sounds "Whish, whish, whoo."

Example 2

> WHO HAS SEEN THE WIND?
>
> NEITHER YOU NOR I;
>
> BUT WHEN I HEAR "WHISH, WHISH, WHOO,"
>
> THE WIND IS PASSING BY.

2 **Who or what makes the sounds "Whish, whish, whoo" in this poem?**

  A   the person called "I" in the poem

  B   the person called "you" in the poem

  C   the poet

  D   the wind

 Your teacher will discuss your answer.

POETIC LANGUAGE

Writers, and especially poets, often use words in a special way. When they use words and phrases in this way, we say that they are using **figurative language**.

Read Example 3. Look at the language the author uses to describe a cloud.

Example 3

> The cloud swelled up like a giant sponge filled with water. Then the rain came down. It sounded as though nails were being pounded into metal.

In this passage, the writer compares a cloud to a sponge filled with water. Instead of saying it was a rain cloud, the writer uses poetic language to get our attention.

Read the passage again and then answer the question.

3 **When you read that the rain "sounded as though nails were being pounded into metal," you can guess that the rain**

    A   was very quiet

    B   was loud

    C   made everyone happy

    D   was like a lullaby

Choice B is correct. If the rain sounded like nails being hammered into metal, it was loud.

HELPFUL HINTS FOR UNDERSTANDING POETRY

1. Poetry takes careful reading.

2. When you read a poem:

- ask yourself who is speaking (is it the poet or someone else?)
- ask yourself what the poem is mainly about. Often, the title will give you a clue.
- ask yourself what the poem says about life. Does it have a theme or lesson about life?
- use context clues to understand what the author means.

SELECTIONS FOR PRACTICE

Selection 1

> SADLY, STEVIE SITS UP IN BED
>
> AND RAISES HIS HAND TO HIS SLEEPY HEAD.
>
> TODAY IS SUNDAY, THE VERY LAST DAY
>
> BEFORE LESSONS BEGIN BACK AT HAMPTON BAY.
>
> THE BEACH, THE SAND, THE SEA WAS FUN.
>
> SEEMS THE HOLIDAY HAS JUST BEGUN.
>
> BUT NOW, TOO SOON, THEY MUST PACK AND GO
>
> BACK TO THE HOUSES THAT STAND ALL IN A ROW.

1   **The main idea of this poem is that**

- ○   Stevie and his family live near the ocean
- ○   Stevie doesn't want his vacation to end
- ○   Stevie has to travel a long way to get to school
- ○   Stevie can't wait to go back to school

Selection 2

TWO BOYS

BY HEATHER FLAME

THE CITY BOY WALKED DOWN THE STREET

AND LAUGHED AT THE PEOPLE HE DID MEET.

THE COUNTRY LAD WALKED PAST THE FARM

AND LAUGHED BECAUSE THE COWS WERE CALM.

AND IF THE TWO OF THEM CHANGE PLACES,

WILL ONE LAUGH AT PIGS AND THE OTHER AT FACES?

2A **What is this poem mostly about?**

- O a city boy who walks through the city
- O a country boy who lives on a farm
- O two boys who like to laugh
- O how to have fun in the country

2B **Who is speaking in the poem?**

- O the city boy
- O the country boy
- O both boys
- O the poet

Selection 3

THE SQUIRREL

WHISKY, FRISKY
HIPPITY HOP,
UP HE GOES
TO THE TREE TOP!
WHIRLY, TWIRLY
ROUND AND ROUND,
DOWN HE SCAMPERS
TO THE GROUND.
FURLY, CURLY,
WHAT A TAIL!
TALL AS A FEATHER,
BROAD AS A SAIL!
WHERE'S HIS SUPPER?
IN THE SHELL,
SNAPPITY, CRACKITY,
OUT IT FELL!

3A **Which of these words describes the squirrel's tail?**

- O   furly, curly
- O   whisky, frisky
- O   hippity hop
- O   snappity, crackity

3B **What do the words "whirly, twirly" describe?**

- O   how the squirrel turns round and round
- O   how the squirrel digs in the ground
- O   what the squirrel's ears are like
- O   how the squirrel eats

Sometimes you will be asked to pick the sentence that completes a passage best. Before you choose the sentence, be sure to read the sentences that come before and after the blank.

Read this passage. Then pick the sentence that belongs in the blank.

Example 1

Everyone in our class likes games. _____.
Others like Hangman more.

1   **Pick the sentence that fits *best* in the blank.**

    A   Our class has 25 students.

    B   Some students like Word Search best.

    C   Word Search is not hard to play.

    D   The teacher usually keeps score when we play Word Search.

Choice B is correct. If you read the first and last sentence, you can figure out that this sentence is the one that MOST belongs in the blank.

The first sentence in the paragraph tells the main idea—that "Everyone in our class likes to play games." The last sentence gives a supporting detail. It says that "Others like games like Hangman more." The word *others* gives you a clue that the missing sentence should tell about what game *some* students in the class like to play.

Read Example 2 and decide which sentence *best* completes the paragraph.

Example 2

Porcupines are small and slow-moving animals. They have a good way of protecting themselves. _____.

Porcupine

2 **Pick the sentence that fits *best* in the blank.**

A Porcupines live in the forest.

B They have brownish-black fur.

C They have sharp quills that stick in any animal that attacks them.

D Porcupines eat plants and tree bark.

Choice C is correct. It is the only sentence that tells something about how porcupines protect themselves. It completes the passage.

Other times you will be asked to pick the sentence that is the best beginning to a passage or story.

Read the next example and answer the question.

Example 3

_____ She looked at the water. Then she dived in.

3 **Find the *best* first sentence for this paragraph.**

A Tina swam as fast as she could.

B Tina got to the beach early.

C Tina loves going to the circus.

D Tina dried off.

Choice B is the best answer. You can figure out that the other choices don't fit. The second sentence says that Tina looked at the water. The third sentence says she dove in. The first thing that Tina would have done was to get to the beach. The other choices don't make sense.

HELPFUL HINTS
FOR CHOOSING THE BEST SENTENCE

1. When you are asked to pick the best sentence, read the sentences before and after the blank.

2. When you are asked to pick the best sentence at the beginning of the passage, make sure you choose one that happens before the other sentences.

3. When you choose the best last sentence, make sure you choose the sentence that happens last or the sentence that makes the most sense.

4. When you choose the best sentence, look for word clues in the other sentences that tell you which sentence is the best choice.

SELECTIONS FOR PRACTICE

Selection 1

Jason and I went to the movies yesterday. _____. Jason wanted to see it again.

1 **Pick the sentence that fits *best* in the blank.**

- O   The popcorn had too much butter.
- O   Jason played basketball until midnight.
- O   The movie was all about outer space.
- O   Jason's teacher doesn't have a cold anymore.

Selection 2

Alice played tennis all afternoon. Then she was very hungry. _____.

2 **Pick the sentence that fits *best* in the blank.**

- O   She always tries to win every point.
- O   She does her homework at night.
- O   She likes to swim, too.
- O   She ate three cheeseburgers with a lot of fries.

Selection 3

_____. Goats like to eat grass, the leaves of plants, fruits, and vegetables the best. They will also eat paper and string. Some people think they even eat tin cans, but this isn't true.

3 **Pick the sentence that fits *best* in the blank.**

- O   Cave men drew pictures of goats.
- O   Some goats have horns.
- O   Some people drink goat's milk.
- O   Goats eat many different things.

■

PART 4: WRITING

16 WRITING TO A PROMPT

Your teacher will ask you to write one long piece. You will be asked to write a letter or a composition or some other kind of long, written answer.

This section will help you write a long answer. It will show you some ways to answer a question like this one:

> What was the strangest dream you ever had? Explain what made it so strange.

DEVELOPING A CENTRAL IDEA

Your first task in answering a question like this is to select a dream that you remember. Usually you start by thinking about different dreams you have had. You need to keep thinking until you come up with one that was strange AND that you can remember well enough to describe.

Once you have remembered a dream, you must decide what made it so strange.

Imagine your friend Ashley remembers a dream where she was lost.

Let's see her tell what made her dream so strange.

> What was the strangest dream you ever had? Explain what made it so strange.

Ashley's Answer

This was my dream. I went into the supermarket. I went to the vegetable part and picked up two ripe bananas and a large cabbage. Then I left the store and walked back towards school. The things that made the dream strange were first, I wasn't afraid, even though I was so little. Why did I choose a cabbage? I don't even like cabbage. And it's a puzzle why I would take a cabbage to school. I was hungry so I ate one of the bananas right there in the store.

There was a little boy in the store who was lost. He was crying. I didn't know what to do. Then he stopped crying and started to laugh. I couldn't understand why.

It was a very hot day. I was so hot I didn't know what to do. That's why I went into the supermarket. It was much cooler there. I was by myself. I was about six years old.

This is quite a good answer. Ashley describes her dream well. She gives supporting details to explain what made it so strange. But she has not organized her answer very well. In the next two sections you will learn some tips for organizing your answer.

PLANNING YOUR WRITING

If you have a lot of information you want to write about, you may want to make a list. Then you can put your ideas in order. If you are writing about a dream or an event, you can arrange your ideas in time order. Start with what happened first, then next, and on to the last event. At the end, you can write what you thought of the dream or the event.

Ashley could have made a list like this one. She could have begun with the events of the dream. She could have put them in time order. Then she could have written about what made the dream strange.

Events that happened in the dream:

1. It was a very hot day. I went to the supermarket to get cool. I was about six years old.

2. I went to the vegetable part. I bought bananas and cabbage. I ate the bananas in the store.

3. A little boy was lost in the store. He was crying. Then he stopped crying and began laughing. I didn't understand why.

4. I left the store and walked toward school.

Why the dream was strange:

1. I wasn't afraid to go to the supermarket by myself even though I was only 6 years old.

2. I don't know why I bought a cabbage because I don't even like cabbage. I don't know why I brought the cabbage to school.

ORGANIZING YOUR WRITING

There are many ways to organize a written answer. One good way is to write your answer in three parts.

> The first part is an opening sentence or two. In these sentences, you can tell the reader what you are writing about.

> The second part is the main part of the answer. You can describe events or tell a story or give facts about a topic in this part.

> The closing sentences sum up what you have said. They could also tell your own thoughts and ideas about the events or topic.

What you include in each part depends on the kind of answer or essay you are writing.

If you are asked to *explain why something happened*, you will begin by stating what that something is. You will list why it happened in the main part of the paper. Then you will end by telling your ideas about what you have written.

Let's go back to the topic from the start of this section:

> What was the strangest dream you ever had? Explain what made it so strange.

Rewrite Ashley's answer using the list of events on page 126. Remember to include the information telling what made the dream so strange.

Make sure your answer has one or two opening sentences, a main part, and a closing or summing up part.

QUESTION FOR PRACTICE

Now it's your turn to answer this question in writing.

> What was the strangest dream *you* ever had? Explain what made it so strange.

Use the page labeled **Planning** to write notes or to make a list of things you want to say.

Use the lines labeled **Writing** to write your essay.

When you finish, go back and reread your essay. Make any changes you want to make neatly on your composition or rewrite your composition on the lines labeled **Rewriting**.

You are not told to write your answer in cursive. That means that you can print or write.

Planning

Writing

_____

_____

_____

_____

_____

_____

_____

_____

_____

_____

_____

_____

_____

_____

_____

_____

_____

_____

_____

_____

_____

_____

_____

_____

_____

_____

_____

_____

_____

_____

_____

_____

_____

_____

_____

_____

Checking

Look back over what you wrote. Answer these questions.

- Did you begin with a sentence or two telling about your topic?
- Did you tell about your dream in the order in which things happened?
- Did you end by telling why the dream was strange?
- Did you write so that it is easy to follow?
- Did you choose your words carefully to express your ideas?
- Did you write in complete sentences? Did each sentence begin with a capital letter and end with a period or question mark?
- Did you check your spelling?

Now go back and make any changes you need to.

Correct your essay neatly. You can rewrite your essay on the lines labeled Rewriting if you wish.

Rewriting

_____

_____

_____

_____

_____

_____

_____

_____

_____

_____

_____

_____

_____

_____

_____

_____

_____

17 USING CORRECT GRAMMAR AND PUNCTUATION

When you finish your writing, you must check it carefully.

These are some things you should check:

- Did you write in complete sentences?
- Did you spell all words correctly?
- Did you use capital letters where needed?
- Did you use commas and end marks correctly in your sentences?

In this chapter, we will go over the most important rules to remember if you want your writing to be correct.

PUNCTUATION

End Marks

There are three marks to use at the end of a sentence.

(.)   the **period**, used after most sentences:

> Jesse looked at the toad.

(?)   the **question mark**, used after questions:

> What time is it?

(!)   the **exclamation point**, used to show strong feelings or after strong commands to do something:

> Our team won! I'm so happy!
> Don't do that! Put it down!

Example 1

1 **Which sentence has the wrong punctuation?**

A   Are you going to Alan's house today?

B   Watch out for that slippery ice!

C   They walked slowly down the street.

D   Where is my baseball jacket.

Choice D has the wrong punctuation. It is a question. It needs a question mark.

Example 2

2 **Which sentence has the correct punctuation?**

O   Stop doing that right now!

O   Stop doing that right now?

O   Will you please answer my question.

O   I knew the answers to all the questions

 Your teacher will discuss your answer.

Commas

When you write a letter, you must use commas in these places:

- in the date
  Put a comma after the day of the month.

    March 23, 2001

- in the greeting
  The greeting is the "hello" part of a letter.
  Put a comma after the person's name.

    Dear Tommy,

- in the closing
  The closing is the "goodbye" part of a letter.
  Put a comma after the closing and before you sign your name.

    Your friend,
        Ricky

    Your son,
        Ricky

    Yours truly,
        Richard Haber

- Put a comma between the name of the town or city and the state.
  When you write an address on the envelope, it should look like this.

    Miss Paula Rullo
    836 Winding Brook Drive
    Indianapolis, Indiana 46234

Example 3

3   **Which choice shows commas used correctly?**

A   January, 24, 2002

B   Dear Michael

C   Yours truly,
Lois McCarthy

D   Your friend
Carlos

Only Choice C is correct. There is a comma after the closing (*Yours truly,*) and before the person's signed name.

All the other choices have mistakes. Choice A has a wrong comma after the name of the month. Choice B has no comma after the greeting. Choice D has no comma after the closing.

Example 4

4   **Which sentence does NOT use the comma correctly?**

O   Dear Mrs. Swenson,

O   November 14, 2000

O   Your sister
Serena

O   Yours truly,
Serena Apostal

 Your teacher will discuss your answer.

Apostrophes

Apostrophes are used to replace missing letters in a contraction. A **contraction** is one word made from two longer ones. An **apostrophe** takes the place of the missing letters in the contraction.

WORDS		CONTRACTION
I am	=	I'm
it is	=	it's
you are	=	you're
do not	=	don't
she will	=	she'll

Apostrophes are also used to show possession, or ownership, of something:

Bill's house

Latisha's sister

Mr. Chang's opinion

Example 5

5 **Which sentence has a mistake in the use of an apostrophe?**

    A   Ill meet you at the movies at noon.

    B   There's someone at the door to see you.

    C   You're invited to my birthday party.

    D   We haven't finished our chores yet.

Choice A does not use the apostrophe correctly. *I'll* is a contraction of *I* and *will*. It should be written *I'll*. All the other contractions have the apostrophe in the right place.

Example 6

6 **Which sentence does NOT use the apostrophe correctly?**

○   Javier doesn't like to play softball.

○   Lets surprise Mom and clean our rooms.

○   It's a beautiful day to be outdoors.

○   They're coming to our house tomorrow.

 Your teacher will discuss your answer.

CAPITAL LETTERS

The first word in a sentence always begins with a capital letter.

An apple a day keeps the doctor away.

The word "I" always begins with a capital letter.

I'm glad I went to see that movie.

These words always begin with capital letters:

Names of people:

James W. Riley

General William Henry Harrison

Ms. Stacy Anderson

Names of places:

South Bend   New Castle
Lake Michigan   Brown County
Fort Wayne   Wabash River
Hoosier National Forest   Jefferson Street Bridge

Names of days of the week, the months, and holidays:

Tuesday   August   Fourth of July   Memorial Day

The first word in the closing of a letter:

Your friend,   Sincerely yours,

Do NOT capitalize the names of the seasons.

spring   summer   fall   winter

Example 7

7   **Which sentence does NOT use capital letters correctly?**

A   Tammy Blake was born in Indianapolis, Indiana.

B   Columbus day is on a Thursday this year.

C   Frank and his family went to the Lincoln Memorial.

D   We visited Wyandotte Cave in June.

Choice B has a mistake. Both words in "Columbus Day" need capitals.

Example 8

8   **Which sentence does NOT use capitals correctly?**

O   Merle Brown lives in Fargo, North Dakota.

O   Hawaii and Japan are in the Pacific Ocean.

O   Valentine's Day is in February.

O   Salt Lake city is near the Great Salt Lake in Utah.

Your teacher will discuss your answer.

SENTENCES

Writing Complete Sentences

Your writing must be in *complete sentences.*

Here are some groups of words that are NOT complete sentences.

> Three clowns in the circus
>
> Have seat belts
>
> To the movies

None of these word groups has both a subject and a verb. None of them is a sentence, so none of them should end with a period.

Another group of words begins with words like *after, before, if, when, since,* and other joining words:

> After the party is over
>
> If you don't want to

Even though these groups of words have a subject and a verb that agrees with it, they are NOT complete sentences. They are not complete because they do not express a complete thought.

Pick out the group of words that is NOT a complete sentence in Example 9.

Example 9

> Juanita wants to be a figure skater. Like Tara Lipinski. She takes skating lessons. Every day after school, she practices at the skating rink.

9   **Which is NOT a complete sentence?**

    A   Juanita wants to be a figure skater.

    B   Like Tara Lipinski.

    C   She takes skating lessons.

    D   Every day after school, she practices at the skating rink.

Choice B, *Like Tara Lipinski*, is NOT a complete sentence because it doesn't have a subject and a verb. To fix this, you would combine the first and second sentences to read: *Juanita wants to be a figure skater like Tara Lipinski.*

Example 10

(1) The dinner dishes have not been washed. (2) There are dirty pots on the stove. (3) Mom and Dad are going to be very angry. (4) When they get home.

10 **Which is NOT a complete sentence?**

- 1
- 2
- 3
- 4

Run-On Sentences

Here are two complete sentences that have been run together into one sentence. This kind of sentence is called a **run-on**.

The flowers are blooming the grass is green.

One way to correct the run-on is to make it into two sentences:

The flowers are blooming. The grass is green.

Example 11

(1) Spring is here. (2) The cherry trees have pink blossoms. (3) Flowers are growing in the yard. (4) The birds are back they are eating seeds at the bird feeder.

11 **Which is a run-on sentence?**

A   1
B   2
C   3
D   4

The correct answer is D. This run-on sentence should be made into two sentences: *The birds are back. They are eating seeds at the bird feeder.*

Example 12

12 **Which choice is written correctly?**

O   Alice was hungry, she was waiting for supper.

O   Alice was hungry she was waiting for supper.

O   Alice was hungry. she was waiting for supper.

O   Alice was hungry. She was waiting for supper.

NOTICE: Photocopying any part of this book is forbidden by law.

143

MAKING SUBJECTS AND VERBS AGREE

When you write a sentence, you must make sure that the verb "agrees" or "goes with" the subject. For example:

CORRECT:	**I am** here.
	(The word *am* always goes with the word *I*).
INCORRECT:	**I is** here.
	(The word *is* doesn't go with the word *I*).

CORRECT:	**The cat chases** mice.
INCORRECT:	**The cat chase** mice.
	(Can you see what's wrong?)

In the sentence:

The cat chases mice.

The cat is one thing, so it is a **singular** subject.

This is how the verb changes when there is more than one cat, when the subject is **plural**.

The cats chase mice.

In other words, in the same sentence, *both* the subject and verb must be plural *or* singular. "Chase" is the plural verb. "Chases" is the singular verb.

If you use a pronoun in place of a noun, make sure it agrees with the verb. Use the pronoun "it" for one thing. Use the pronoun "they" for more than one thing.

It chases mice.

They chase mice.

Example 13

13 **In which sentence does the verb NOT agree with the subject?**

    A   Karen knits sweaters for her dolls.

    B   The children have new clothes.

    C   Terry and Dennis enjoys basketball.

    D   The lion walks through the jungle.

Choice C has the mistake. Two boys are the subject of this sentence. The verb should also be plural. The correct way to write the sentence is: *Terry and Dennis enjoy basketball*. In all the other choices, the subject "goes" or "agrees with" the verb.

Example 14

14 **In which sentence do the subject and verb NOT agree?**

    O   She does not like that television show.

    O   Most animals has a way to hide from danger.

    O   Many birds fly south every winter.

    O   Lizards do not make good pets.

VERB TENSES

The **tense** of a verb shows when something happened: *today, tomorrow, yesterday.* Here are the most often used tenses of a verb.

Present Tenses:

I (you, we, *or* they) try   she (he *or* it) tries
I am trying   she (he *or* it) is trying
you (we *or* they) are trying

Future Tense:

I (you, she, he, we, *or* they) will try

Past Tenses:

I (you, we, *or* they) tried
she (he *or* it) has tried   we (you *or* they) have tried

Example 15

15 **In which sentence is the verb used correctly?**

    A   I seen the basketball game last night.

    B   We been learning a new dance.

    C   She will be acting in the school play.

    D   The flowers grew and bloom.

Choice C is correct. Choice A is incorrect because the verb should be "saw." In Choice B, the verb should be "have been learning." In Choice D, the two verbs should be in the same tense: the past. The sentence should read: *The flowers grew and bloomed.*

Example 16

The cat _____ the tree right now.

16 **Find the word or words that best complete the sentence.**

- ○ is climbing
- ○ are climbing
- ○ climbing
- ○ climbed

Read the sentences. Look at the number given to each sentence. Answer the questions below.

Selection 1

(1) Some people think that goats will eat anything, this is not true. (2) Goats like grass, the leaves of plants, fruits, and vegetables best. (3) But they will eat paper, string, and tin cans. (4) They don't really like tin cans. (5) They eat the label. (6) For the glue on it. (7) If you own a goat, feed it good food that it likes.

1 **Which is NOT a complete sentence?**

- ○ Sentence 4
- ○ Sentence 5
- ○ Sentence 6
- ○ Sentence 7

2 **Which is a run-on sentence?**

- ○ Sentence 1
- ○ Sentence 2
- ○ Sentence 6
- ○ Sentence 7

Selection 2

Karen wrote this letter to her friend Jill. Think about what changes need to be made to the underlined sentences. Then answer the questions.

June 2, 2000

Dear Jill

I have some very exciting news! Mom, Dad, Billy, and I are going to Yellowstone national park in July. We would like you to come with us. Do you think you can, i hope so. We will have so much fun.

I knows some great things to see at the park. Lots of animals live there. Dad said we can fish in Yellowstone Lake. We can see hot springs that shoot up in the air. One is called Old Faithful. It shoots water into the air every 78 minutes. We has to time it just right to get there when it goes off.

I almost forgot to tell you the most exciting part. We are going to camp out in the park. Well sleep in a tent and cooking our food over a campfire. We can roast marshmallows over the fire and sing songs. I can hardly wait! Write back soon and tell me if you can come.

your friend

Karen

3   <u>June 2, 2000</u> should be written

- ○   June, 2, 2000,
- ○   June 2, 2000,
- ○   June 2 2000
- ○   Do not change.

4   <u>Dear Jill</u> should be written

- ○   dear Jill,
- ○   Dear Jill,
- ○   Dear jill
- ○   Do not change.

5   In Sentence 2, <u>Yellowstone national park in July</u> should be written

- ○   Yellowstone National park in July
- ○   Yellowstone National Park in July
- ○   Yellowstone national park in july
- ○   Do not change.

6   In Sentence 4, <u>Do you think you can, i hope so</u> should be written

- ○   Do you think you can. i hope so.
- ○   Do you think you can. I hope so.
- ○   Do you think you can? I hope so.
- ○   Do not change.

7   In Sentence 6, <u>I knows</u> should be written

- ○   I know
- ○   I am knowing
- ○   I will know
- ○   Do not change.

8   In Sentence 12, <u>We has to time it just right</u> should be written

- ○   We are having to time it just right
- ○   We have to time it just right
- ○   We having to time it just right
- ○   Do not change.

9   Sentence 15 , <u>Well sleep in a tent and cooking our food over a campfire</u>, should be written

- ○   We'll sleep in a tent and cook our food over a campfire.
- ○   We'll sleep in a tent and cooked our food over a campfire.
- ○   We'll sleep in a tent and cooks our food over a campfire.
- ○   Do not change.

10   The closing <u>your friend Karen</u> should be written

- ○   your friend, Karen
- ○   Your Friend, Karen
- ○   Your friend, Karen
- ○   Do not change.

18 USING CORRECT SPELLING

Here are some tips to help you spell better.

- When you do your homework or do any writing, be sure you have a dictionary handy. Use it to check the spelling of any words you are not sure of.

- If you spell a word wrong in class or in your homework, find the correct spelling as soon as you can.

- If you use a computer or a word processor, find out if it has a spell checker. If it does, use it.

Your teacher may give you words to learn each week. This will add to the number of words you can spell. Reading does the same thing. The more you read, the more words you will see spelled correctly.

Many words sound the same but are spelled differently. Here you can see how some of these word pairs are used:

Bread is made with **flour**.	The **flower** in the vase is a rose.
Let's meet at **four** o'clock.	Kevin played piano **for** an hour.
Did you **hear** Crystal sing?	The guests will be **here** very soon.
The puppy dug a **hole**.	Grandma cooked a **whole** turkey.
It's fun to draw with markers.	The kitten licked **its** fur.
Miguel **knew** all the answers.	Her **new** bike was shiny and red.
There are many cars on the **road**.	Iris **rode** a white horse.
We swam in the blue **sea**.	Did you **see** the movie about whales?
It is **so** hot in this room!	Michelle loves to **sew**.

Danny is older **than** I am.

Their father is my teacher.

We enjoyed our trip **to** Virginia.

You're my best friend.

They ate lunch and **then** went home.

Put the package down over **there**.

They're going to move to Washington.

We visited Maryland, **too**.

I traveled with my **two** cousins.

Open **your** present right now!

Learn as many of the word pairs as you can. Then try the practice questions.

QUESTIONS FOR PRACTICE

Read the sentences. Fill in the bubble beneath any word that is spelled wrong. If a sentence has no wrong words, then circle the bubble under No error.

1 <u>There</u> are <u>flowers</u> and <u>vegtables</u> in our garden. <u>No error</u>.
   O   O   O   O

2 The <u>butterflys</u> are <u>so</u> <u>beautiful</u>! <u>No error</u>.
     O   O O   O

3 A <u>clowd</u> <u>floated</u> across the <u>summer</u> sky. <u>No error</u>.
   O   O   O   O

4 Each <u>child</u> <u>wore</u> <u>mittens</u>. <u>No error</u>.
     O   O   O   O

5 Did you <u>here</u> the <u>silly</u> joke she told <u>today</u>? <u>No error</u>.
      O   O   O   O

6 The puppy <u>wagged</u> <u>it's</u> <u>tail</u>. <u>No error</u>.
        O   O O   O

7 <u>They're</u> <u>sitting</u> on the <u>bench</u>. <u>No error</u>.
   O   O   O   O

8 The <u>little</u> dog <u>barked</u> at the <u>bigest</u> one. <u>No error</u>.
     O   O   O   O

9 Dad likes to <u>drive</u> on the <u>rode</u> in his <u>new</u> car. <u>No error</u>.
       O   O   O   O

10 I went <u>to</u> the <u>movies</u> and <u>than</u> went home. <u>No error</u>.
     O   O   O   O

PART 5: READING AND LANGUAGE ARTS REVIEW AND ASSESSMENT

In this section, you will read stories and sentences. Then you will answer questions about them. The questions will be like those you answered earlier in this book.

Read the selection.

Then read each question.

Then look carefully at the answer choices. Sometimes there are four and sometimes only three. Pick the best answer.

You can look back at the selection as much as you want. This will help you pick the right answer.

Here are some practice questions. Read each one. Then pick the best answer. Fill in the bubble under the best answer. Remember to fill in the whole bubble. Make your marks dark.

PRACTICE A

The cat saw the bird on the ground. She wanted to catch the bird. But then something made the cat run away. Find the picture that shows what made the cat run away.

a flower	a dog	a bird
O	O	O

PRACTICE B

Find the words that best complete the sentence.

Our team _____.

baseball stars	won the game	at school	in the morning
O	O	O	O

REVIEW 1: READING AND LANGUAGE ARTS

THEME:
A WORLD OF SURPRISES

THE WORLD IS AN EXCITING PLACE. THERE ARE MANY INTERESTING THINGS TO SEE. THERE ARE LOTS OF NEW THINGS TO FIND OUT ABOUT. NEXT, YOU WILL READ SOME STORIES ABOUT THE SURPRISES YOU MIGHT FIND.

Directions
This poem is about a kitten that a child sees in a tree. She is surprised to see the kitten, and it is surprised to see her. Read the poem. Then answer questions 1 through 6.

OUT THE WINDOW
BY PAMELA DEAN

I LOOKED OUT THE WINDOW, AND WHAT DID I SEE?

TWO LITTLE EYES STARING BACK AT ME.

I STARED AT IT, AND IT STARED AT ME.

I IN MY ROOM AND IT IN THE TREE.

IT WAS SO CLOSE, I COULD ALMOST FEEL

HOW SOFT IT WOULD BE, AND OH, SO REAL.

AS I STRETCHED MY HAND OUT INTO THE DAY

SADLY, I WATCHED IT SCAMPER AWAY.

GO ON

1 **Where is the child when she sees the kitten?**

- ○ in the tree
- ○ in the garden
- ○ in her room

2 **In the poem, the child says, "I stared at it and it stared at me." Who is *it*?**

- ○ another child
- ○ a kitten
- ○ a bird

3 **What does the child try to do to the kitten?**

- ○ She tries to pet the kitten.
- ○ She tries to chase the kitten away.
- ○ She tries to feed the kitten.

4 **How does the child feel about the kitten?**

- ○ She does not like it.
- ○ She likes it a lot.
- ○ She is afraid of it.

5 **Why does the kitten run away?**

- ○ It is afraid of the girl.
- ○ It is hungry.
- ○ It sees another kitten.

6 **The girl watched the kitten *scamper* away. Which choice means the same as *scamper*?**

- ○ yell loudly
- ○ run quickly
- ○ play happily

GO ON

Directions
This story is about a surprising trip. Read the story. Then answer questions 7 through 13.

THE WISH TREE

The class went on a trip. They went to Mr. Green's farm in North Terra Haute. There is a very old oak tree on the farm. It is called "The Wish Tree."

You sit next to the tree, close your eyes, and make a wish. Then you throw a dime near the tree. Mr. Green says your wish will come true.

Manuel and his sister Rosa sat next to the tree. They closed their eyes and threw their dimes next to the tree.

Manuel wished for a baseball bat. Rosa wanted a pair of roller blades. Manuel didn't get a bat for his birthday. Instead he got a book and new sneakers. He said he thought the tree was deaf. He wants his dime back. But Rosa smiled when she saw her gift. She got a new pair of fast roller blades.

Rosa loves the Wish Tree. She says it should be called "The Happiness Tree." She hopes her class goes back to Mr. Green's farm. Next time Rosa is going to wish for a mountain bike.

GO ON

7 What is *supposed* to happen when you throw a dime near "The Wish Tree"?

- ○ You win a lot of money.
- ○ Your wish comes true.
- ○ You can come back to the farm.

8 Manuel *didn't* get a bat for his birthday. What is another way to say *didn't*?

- ○ did not
- ○ did never
- ○ did want

9 How does Manuel feel when he gets the book and sneakers?

- ○ He is not happy.
- ○ He is very happy.
- ○ He likes them as much as a bat.

10 Why does Manuel say he thinks the tree is deaf?

deaf = unable to hear

- ○ The tree has no ears.
- ○ The tree gave his sister her wish.
- ○ The tree did not give him his wish.

11 Why does Rosa call the tree "The Happiness Tree"?

- ○ It is a beautiful tree.
- ○ She got her wish.
- ○ She loves trees.

12 Mr. Green tells Manuel to make another wish at "The Wish Tree." What does Manuel probably say?

- ○ "Yes. This time I will get my wish."
- ○ "No. It doesn't work."
- ○ "I don't want a bat anymore."

13 Which action happened in the past?

- ○ The class went on a trip.
- ○ Rosa is going to wish for a mountain bike.
- ○ Manuel wants his dime back.

GO ON

Directions

This story is about a girl named Ginny. She goes to the beach and has a surprise. Read the story and then answer questions 14 through 21.

A TRIP TO THE BEACH

Ginny lived near Lake Michigan. She loved to go to the beach and swim in the lake. She loved the summer but she detested the winter. All through the long, cold months, she waited for the snow to melt. She wished for spring and summer to come.

Today was the first really warm day of the year. Ginny's mother was taking her to the beach. They packed their car with beach things. They brought a blanket, a swimming tube, some snacks, and water. Ginny's mother brought a book to read, and Ginny packed some toys.

When they got there, they stood looking at the crowded beach. Ginny was surprised that there were so many people there. "I'll go ahead and get us a spot," her mother said. "Why don't you buy yourself an ice cream cone?"

Ginny went over to the stand and asked for a chocolate cone. Chocolate was her favorite flavor. She started eating the ice cream slowly. It tasted so good. She was pleased to be at the beach. As she walked toward the beach, Ginny looked at the big puffy clouds in the sky. When she got to the sand, she took off her sandals. It felt great to push her toes into the warm sand.

ice cream cone

GO ON

Ginny was so busy enjoying the sand that she didn't see a little boy running towards her. Before she could get out of his way, he crashed into her. She fell down and dropped her cone. It was covered with sand. Ginny was about to cry, but she laughed instead. It was too nice a day to be sad. Besides, the cone looked funny sitting upside down in the sand.

14 **What is this story mostly about?**

- O   a girl who likes clouds and sailboats
- O   a girl's first trip to the beach in the summer
- O   a girl who buys an ice cream cone

15 **Ginny loved summer, but she *detested* winter. What does *detested* mean?**

- O   forgot
- O   enjoyed
- O   hated

16 **Mom says, "*I'll* go ahead and get us a spot."**
What is another way to say "*I'll*"?

- O   I should
- O   I will
- O   I can

17 **Ginny dropped her cone because**

- O   it was too cold to hold
- O   she had finished the ice cream
- O   a little boy bumped into her

18 **What happened after Ginny dropped her cone?**

- O   She was hit by a little boy.
- O   She was about to cry.
- O   She took off her sandals.

GO ON

19 **Why did Ginny laugh when she saw her ice cream cone in the sand?**

○ She thought the ice cream cone looked funny.

○ She always laughed when things went wrong.

○ She thought the boy was funny.

20 **Which of these is an *opinion*?**

○ Summer is warm.

○ Snow melts.

○ Chocolate is the best flavor.

21 **Which set of words best completes the sentence below?**

The beach _____.

○ full of people

○ crowded with people

○ was crowded

GO ON

Directions
What do you think of bats? You may be surprised when you read this selection about bats. Read the selection. Then answer questions 22-30.

A bat looks like a mouse with wings. Bats can fly. But bats are not birds. They don't have feathers.

Bats don't like sunlight. They sleep during the day. They search for food at night.

Bats eat fruits and bugs. They can catch flying bugs at night. They can hunt even when it's dark. An insect may twist and turn. But the insect doesn't get away. Bats are good hunters. They have to be because they need to eat many, many insects every night.

Bats often live in caves. Thousands of bats live in one cave. In the evening, they all leave their cave at the same time. If you look up, you see them everywhere. The sky is full of bats.

Most animals sleep lying down. Some animals sleep standing up. But bats are different. They hang upside down. Their heads face the ground.

Many people are scared of bats. They are afraid bats will fly in their hair. But this doesn't happen. Most bats stay away from people.

Look at the picture of the bat's face. Some people think the bat has a cute face. But most people think they are ugly.

Some people love bats. But they don't keep bats as pets. Bats are too hard to feed!

GO ON

22 Look at the picture of the bat above. What do you think the bat is doing?

○   hiding from people

○   hunting for food

○   sleeping

23 Bats are NOT like birds because

○   they can't fly

○   they can't hunt for insects

○   they don't have feathers

24 Why do bats hunt at night?

○   They don't like sunlight.

○   They are afraid of people.

○   They are afraid of birds.

25 What does the word *insect* mean in this passage?

○   a bat

○   a bug

○   a piece of fruit

26 How do most animals go to sleep?

○   They hang by their feet.

○   They lie down.

○   They sleep standing up.

27 According to the story, most people

○   are scared of bats

○   keep bats as pets

○   think bats are beautiful

GO ON

28 **Which of these statements is a *fact*?**

- O Bats are beautiful.
- O Bats are scary.
- O Bats sleep upside down.

29 **Bats do not make good pets because**

- O they are hard to catch
- O they are hard to feed
- O they sleep upside down

30 **What detail fits best in the blank space?**

Bats are different from birds. They hunt at night and live in caves. _____.

- O Most birds live in trees and hunt by day.
- O Both birds and bats eat fruit and insects.
- O Bats and birds are very different animals.

REVIEW 2: READING AND LANGUAGE ARTS

THEME:
LIFE CAN BE STRANGE!

IN THIS SECTION, YOU WILL READ ABOUT A NEW THEME, "LIFE CAN BE STRANGE." YOU WILL READ MORE STORIES AND SENTENCES. THEN YOU WILL ANSWER QUESTIONS ABOUT THEM. READ EACH QUESTION. THEN LOOK CAREFULLY AT THE ANSWER CHOICES. IN THIS SECTION, EACH QUESTION WILL HAVE <u>FOUR</u> ANSWER CHOICES.

Here is a practice question. Read the **four** choices. Fill in the bubble under the best answer. Remember to fill in the whole bubble. Make your marks dark.

PRACTICE A

Which of these animals hops instead of walking and eats carrots?

O a dog   O a cat   O a rabbit   O a duck

GO ON

Directions

Sometimes people can be strange. Read about Brian and his adventure. Then answer questions 1 through 5.

Brian loved to climb trees. He climbed every tree in his yard. Yesterday, he and his friend Sam were playing in Sam's yard. Brian saw a great big tree, much bigger than any he had climbed before. "I'm going to climb that tree," he bragged to Sam.

brag = talk big

"I don't think you should try it," Sam said. "That tree is bigger than it looks." Brian just smiled. Then he started to climb the pine tree branch after branch. When he reached the top and looked down, he began to wonder if he could make it down by himself. "I don't think I know how to get back down," he called out to Sam.

Sam ran and got his father and told him that Brian was stuck in the tree. Sam's father got a big ladder and went up to *rescue* Brian. When Brian was finally on the ground again, he told Sam, "I was just joking." He didn't want anyone to know that he was scared. Now Brian thinks twice before he climbs a big tree. He's learned his lesson.

GO ON

1 **What did Brian find out when he got to the top of the tree?**

O   The tree was shorter than he thought.

O   Sam had climbed up after him.

O   Brian couldn't get down from the tree.

O   Sam's father could not help him get down.

2 **Sam's father used a ladder to *rescue* Brian.**

Which word or words mean the same as *rescue*?

O   save

O   speak to

O   look for

O   worry about

3 **Why did Brian say he was just joking?**

O   He wanted to scare Sam by climbing the tree.

O   He wanted to see if Sam's father would save him.

O   He was just pretending to be scared.

O   He didn't want Sam to know he was scared.

4 **Which word means the opposite of *scared*?**

O   bragging

O   wise

O   brave

O   silly

5 **What will *probably* happen if Brian sees a big tree?**

O   He will climb it right away.

O   He will think about climbing it first.

O   He will tell Sam to climb the tree.

O   He will tell Sam's father to cut the tree down.

GO ON

Directions
This selection is about a strange plant called poison ivy. Do you know what it looks like? Read the first part and then answer questions 6 through 8.

Poison ivy is a plant. It grows in many parts of the country. It spreads along the ground. It climbs trees and fences. It grows everywhere.

People who brush against poison ivy get a rash. Their skin itches. It makes them want to scratch. Poison ivy won't kill you. But it makes you feel very unhappy.

A very few people are lucky. They aren't hurt by poison ivy. They never get a rash. But some others need to see a doctor or even go to the hospital.

People often get poison ivy when they walk in the woods. Long sleeves and long pants will help. They *protect* your arms and legs. But it is still easy to get a rash on your fingers or hands.

GO ON

6 Poison ivy makes you unhappy because

- O   it grows on fences
- O   it makes you itch
- O   its leaves change color
- O   it grows everywhere

7 What detail fits best in the blank space?

Poison ivy can do different things to different people. Most people get itchy rashes when they touch poison ivy. _____.

- O   A few people don't get rashes from poison ivy.
- O   Poison ivy grows in the woods.
- O   Poison ivy is a plant.
- O   The woods are dangerous.

8 In the story, *protect* means to

- O   fall over
- O   keep safe
- O   love
- O   remove

GO ON

Directions
Now read more information on poison ivy. Then answer questions 9 through 14.

The best way to recognize poison ivy is by its leaves. They are always found in groups of three. Be careful with any plant with three leaves! In the summer the leaves are a dark, shiny green. They are really quite pretty. But the color changes. In the fall the leaves turn to red or brown.

Don't touch poison ivy. The plant has an oil that gets on your skin. The oil causes the rash. If you touch poison ivy, wash the oil off. Wash as soon as possible with strong soap and water. You must wash for a long time. The oil is hard to wash off.

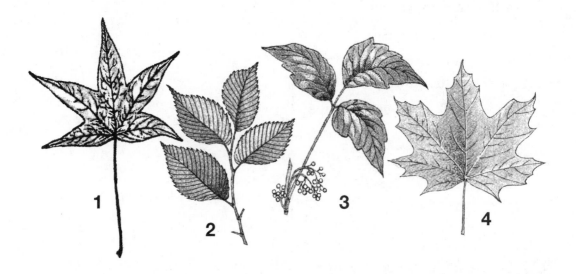

9 **Look at the pictures of the plants. Which one goes with the story?**

O 1   O 2   O 3   O 4

GO ON

NOTICE: Photocopying any part of this book is forbidden by law.

10 Poison ivy has

- O four leaves
- O red flowers
- O one large leaf
- O three leaves

11 Which statement is an *opinion*?

- O Poison ivy has pretty leaves.
- O Poison ivy has shiny, green leaves.
- O Poison ivy leaves change color in fall.
- O Poison ivy leaves have an oil.

12 What should you do after you touch poison ivy?

- O go to the hospital
- O see a doctor
- O wash your skin
- O wear gloves

13 Which word has the same vowel sound as *oil*?

- O boy
- O boat
- O born
- O poem

14 Pick the verb that best fits the sentence.

Last summer my gloves _____ me from poison ivy.

- O protects
- O protecting
- O protected
- O will protect

GO ON

Directions

Here is a story that you might think is strange. It is about two friends, a rabbit and a duck. Read the story and answer questions 15 through 22.

A STRANGE PARTY

Duck decided to have a party. He invited Rabbit to come for tea. "We are going to have delicious cookies, too," Duck told Rabbit.

"Well, thank you, Duck. I'd love to be your guest," said Rabbit.

Rabbit arrived at Duck's house an hour late. "I'm sorry I'm late. I overslept," Rabbit said.

GO ON

"Don't worry," said Duck, as he poured Rabbit a cup of tea. Rabbit hit the cup with his paw by mistake. The tea spilled all over the table.

"Oh, I'm very sorry," said Rabbit. "Let me clean it up." Rabbit tried to wipe the table with his napkin. But he pushed the dishes too hard, and some fell on the ground and broke. "Oh, dear! Oh, dear! I am very, very sorry," Rabbit kept saying, over and over.

"Please don't do any more. I'll clean it up later," Duck said with a sigh. Then Duck told Rabbit to take a cookie. Rabbit took ten big cookies. There were none left for Duck.

Next, Rabbit went into the kitchen where he saw a big carrot cake. "May I have a piece of that?" he asked Duck. Without waiting for an answer, Rabbit ate the whole cake.

Finally it was time for Rabbit to leave. "Well, I'm very full. I guess I should go now," said Rabbit. "This was very nice. I'm not invited out very often." Then Rabbit said to Duck, "Would you like to come out and play with me?"

Duck looked around at the empty cake plate, the broken dishes, and the dirty tablecloth. "No, I don't think so. Having a party is more tiring than I thought."

15 **This story is mostly about**

○ how not to act at a party

○ how to have a good time at a party

○ how to make new friends

○ what to eat at a tea party

16 **Which word best describes Rabbit?**

○ mean

○ sharing

○ careful

○ selfish

GO ON

17 Why does Duck say, "Please don't do any more. I'll clean it up later"?

- O   Duck likes to clean up.
- O   Duck was afraid more dishes would break.
- O   Duck felt sorry for Rabbit.
- O   Duck didn't care about the broken dishes.

18 What was the *first* thing that Rabbit did?

- O   spilled the tea
- O   broke the dishes
- O   arrived late
- O   ate all the goodies

19 How did Duck feel at the end of the story?

- O   tired
- O   happy
- O   worried
- O   not hungry

20 Why doesn't Rabbit get invited out often?

- O   Rabbit doesn't enjoy parties.
- O   Rabbit likes being home best.
- O   Rabbit is a terrible guest.
- O   Rabbit doesn't eat much.

21 This story is probably from a book

- O   of stories about real animals
- O   about make-believe creatures
- O   on facts about animals
- O   that is used to teach science

22 Which word or words best complete this sentence?

Rabbit is the _____ guest Duck ever saw.

- O   ruder
- O   rudest
- O   most rudest
- O   more rude

GO ON

D*irections*
The next selections are about word meanings. Read each selection. One sentence has a blank. Decide which of the answer choices would best fit in the blank.

Try this practice selection.

PRACTICE B

The mother cow played with her calf in the grass. Nearby, a mother cat and her _____ slept in a chair.

    O kitten   O monkey   O bird   O lion

Now do questions 23 through 26.

23 Willy plays baseball during the warm months. In winter, his favorite _____ is basketball.

    O school   O month   O television O sport

24 Carrie works in a hospital. She helps sick people get well again. Carrie is a _____.

    O teacher   O doctor   O friend   O coach

25 During the day, the children swam and played outdoor games. In the _____, they watched the beautiful colors of the sunset.

    O evening O midnight O afternoon O morning

26 You don't need to shout. I can hear you even if you _____.

    O speak   O sing   O whisper   O laugh

GO ON

PRACTICE C

Find the sign that means "POISON."
Fill in the bubble under that sign.

○   ○   ○   ○

27   Find the sign that tells you to stop. Fill in the bubble under that sign.

○   ○   ○   ○

GO ON

28 Find the sign that shows a place where you can cross the road on your bicycle. Fill in the bubble under that sign.

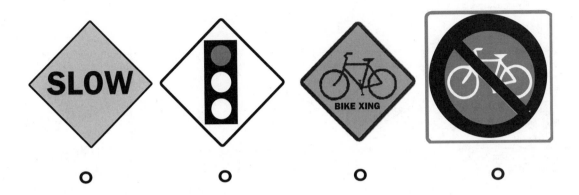

○   ○   ○   ○

Read this list of the hours when a library is open. Then answer question 29.

LIBRARY HOURS

Wednesday, Thursday, Friday	10 A.M. TO 5 P.M.
Tuesday	12 NOON TO 8 P.M.
Saturday	9 A.M. TO 5 P.M.

29 Which day can you go to the library at 9 A.M.?

- ○ Tuesday
- ○ Wednesday
- ○ Friday
- ○ Saturday

GO ON

Read this weather chart. It shows what the weather will be like from Monday to Friday. Then answer question 30.

MONDAY	TUESDAY	WEDNESDAY	THURSDAY	FRIDAY
WARM AND SUNNY	PARTLY CLOUDY	RAINY	CLOUDY	WARM AND SUNNY

30 **Which day will you have to wear a raincoat or carry an umbrella?**

O Tuesday

O Wednesday

O Thursday

O Friday

REVIEW 3: LANGUAGE ARTS AND MECHANICS

PRACTICE A

Each sentence is in three parts. One part may have a mistake. If you find a mistake, fill in the bubble under that part. If there are no mistakes, fill in the bubble under "None."

we saw | a baseball game | in the park. | NONE

   O   O   O   O

Now do Numbers 1 through 3.

1   do you | like to dance | and sing? | NONE

     O   O   O   O

2   They marched | in the parade | on Columbus day. | NONE

     O   O   O   O

3   Danny goes | to soccer practice | every thursday. | NONE

     O   O   O   O

GO ON

PRACTICE B

Read the sentence. Does the sentence need an end mark? If it does, fill in the bubble under the correct end mark. If the sentence already has an end mark, fill in the bubble under "NONE."

The birds are singing

.   ?   NONE

O   O   O

Now do Numbers 4 through 6.

4 **Maria went to the circus.**

!   ?   NONE

O   O   O

5 **Why is the baby crying**

.   ?   NONE

O   O   O

6 **The batter hit the ball**

.   ?   NONE

O   O   O

GO ON

PRACTICE C

Some of these sentences have a mistake. Some do not. Pick the sentence that has NO mistakes. Fill in the bubble next to that sentence.

- O   The cave is full of Bats
- O   Bats are animals with wings
- O   They can fly.
- O   do bats scare you?

Now do Numbers 7 through 10.

7
- O   Sarita runs fast.
- O   Can you run very fast.
- O   My sister runs even faster

8
- O   Flowers bloom in the Spring.
- O   The trees get leaves in April
- O   In June the garden is full of roses.

9
- O   Wont you play with me today?
- O   I do'nt like to play alone.
- O   There aren't many children around.
- O   Ill go get my bicycle.

10
- O   Mrs. Walker is our gym teacher.
- O   Do you like the games we play.
- O   We go to the park on Wednesdays?
- O   Sam doesnt like basketball.

GO ON

PRACTICE D

Pick the choice that has NO mistakes. Fill in the bubble next to that choice.

    ◯   Mr Charles Wallace

    ◯   Mr. Charles Wallace

    ◯   mr charles wallace

    ◯   mr. charles Wallace

Look at the letter. It has blanks with numbers in it. For Numbers 11 through 13, find the choice that has NO mistakes. Fill in the bubble under that choice.

(11)_____

(12)_____

      Can you come to my birthday party next Saturday at 2 in the afternoon? We'll have birthday cake and play lots of games. I hope you can come.

(13)_____

GO ON

11
- ○ May 1 2000
- ○ may 1, 2000
- ○ May, 1, 2000
- ○ May 1, 2000

12
- ○ dear Becky
- ○ Dear becky
- ○ Dear Becky,
- ○ Dear Becky

13
- ○ your friend
- ○ Your friend,
- ○ your friend,
- ○ Your Friend,

GO ON

The next blank is on the envelope for the letter. For Number 14, fill in the bubble next to the answer with NO mistake.

REBECCA MATTHEWS

143 WILLOW LANE

_____

14 O   Brazil Indiana 47834

   O   brazil, indiana 47834

   O   Brazil, Indiana 47834

   O   Brazil, indiana 47834

PRACTICE E

Words are underlined in some of the sentences. Find the answer that CORRECTS the mistake in the underlined part. Fill in the bubble next to this correct answer. If the underlined part has NO mistakes, fill in the bubble next to "Keep as is."

Many birds are at the bird <u>feeder They</u> are eating seeds.

   O   feeder. They

   O   feeder, they

   O   feeder, They

   O   Keep as is.

GO ON

15 Our town has fireworks on <u>Fourth of July</u> every year.

- ○ fourth of July
- ○ Fourth of july
- ○ fourth of july
- ○ Keep as is.

16 My cat <u>Whiskers doesnt</u> like the sound of fireworks.

- ○ whiskers doesn't
- ○ Whiskers doesn't
- ○ Whiskers does'nt
- ○ Keep as is.

17 She runs under the <u>bed she</u> hides there all night.

- ○ bed, she
- ○ bed. She
- ○ bed, She
- ○ Keep as is.

18 Our whole family loves this <u>holiday, we</u> have a picnic every year.

- ○ Holiday. We
- ○ holiday, We
- ○ holiday. We
- ○ Keep as is.

19 The picnic is at Grandma and Grandpa's <u>house everyone bring</u> food.

- ○ house. Everyone bring
- ○ house. everyone
- ○ house. Everyone brings
- ○ Keep as is.

20 <u>They're</u> going to have hot dogs, hamburgers, and lots of desserts.

- ○ Their
- ○ Theyre'
- ○ they're
- ○ Keep as is.

REVIEW 4: WRITING TO A PROMPT

Directions

Read the writing prompt. Then follow the directions to plan and write your answer.

WRITING PROMPT

HAVE YOU EVER THOUGHT WHAT IT WOULD BE LIKE TO BE A BIRD, OR AN ELEPHANT, OR EVEN A SNAKE? CHOOSE AN ANIMAL THAT YOU WOULD LIKE TO BE. WRITE AN ESSAY IN WHICH YOU DESCRIBE WHAT YOUR LIFE WOULD BE LIKE. TELL WHAT YOU WOULD LIKE ABOUT YOUR NEW LIFE.

Use the page labeled **Planning** to make a list of what you will include. Then put your ideas in order. Make your ideas easy for a reader to follow.

Use the lines labeled **Writing** to write your essay.

When you finish, go back and reread your essay. Make any changes you want to make neatly on your essay. If you wish, you can rewrite your essay on the lines labeled **Rewriting**.

188 NOTICE: Photocopying any part of this book is forbidden by law.

Planning

NOTICE: Photocopying any part of this book is forbidden by law.

189

Writing

_____

_____

_____

_____

_____

_____

_____

_____

_____

_____

_____

_____

_____

_____

_____

_____

_____

_____

Checking

Look back over what you wrote. Answer these questions.

- Did you begin with a sentence or two telling about your topic?

- Did you put your ideas in order? Did you write so that it is easy to follow?

- Did you end by summing up what you said?

- Did you choose your words carefully to express your ideas?

- Did you write in complete sentences? Did each sentence begin with a capital letter and end with a period or question mark?

- Did you check your spelling?

Now go back and make any changes you need to.

Correct your essay neatly. You can rewrite your essay on the lines on the next page if you wish.

Rewriting

_____

_____

_____

_____

_____

_____

_____

_____

_____

_____

_____

_____

_____

_____

_____

_____

_____

_____

_____